The message of this book is simply that you can pray, you can meditate, you can contact God. The God of very gods is within you. You can make the contact if you will it so. You can communicate with the Lord even as Moses did—"face to face, as a man speaketh unto his friend."

Who could speak better of the way of prayer than Jesus, the Lord Christ? "Lord, teach us to pray." He is the Saviour, the exemplar, the avatar of this Christian/Piscean age. Jesus is the open door to the individual Christ consciousness—the kingdom of God that is, even now, within you.

"The way of the Christ must be made known and that way is total communion," Jesus says— "continual prayer." Would you experience a limitless flow of strength? of ideas? of abundance? Would you become the arbiter of your own destiny, moving with the gentle winds of the Spirit yet unmoved by the tempest of mass emotion and competitive thought? Would you do something about the mismanagement of our cities, our schools, our money, our freedom? Above all, would you know God? It is a lawful desire. "Through unbroken communion, the life experience of my final embodiment in Galilee and Nazareth can become the forte of every God-realized man."

In your longing, then, to drink deeply of his cup of life, would you pray as the mystics do? Would you feel the fire—would you behold with John the living flame of love? Would you enter with Teresa the Interior Castle? Would you be as Francis and see in the face of the wretched the lightning countenance of the Most High? Come with him, then, on the way of meditation.

"In prayer, man makes intercession to God for assistance," Kuthumi explains. "In meditation, he gives assistance to God by creating the nature of God within his own thoughts and feelings." Kuthumi, the Tibetan mahatma. You may have known him as the Master K.H.

The importance of his teaching on "scientific meditation" lies not only in the demonstration of the nature of light—"where light is, there God is"—or even in the explanation of the seven color rays and the progressive states of consciousness. From K.H., a master psychologist, you may expect to hear of more than the proper disposition of the mind. From the Himalayan adept, you will learn of more than the suitable posture of the body. Albeit he considers both in careful detail. You will discover in meditation with Kuthumi a soul burning with Christic love—a soul 'born again' if you will, 'converted' in the sense of being literally "turned around" in the moment of contact with his own inner Self, the personal Christ.

Empowered by the Holy Spirit, the Messengers Mark and Elizabeth Prophet deliver to new-age disciples of the living Word these teachings on prayer and meditation as entrusted to them by Jesus Christ and his disciple Kuthumi. This one, so well loved as Saint Francis, shares with his Saviour the office of World Teacher yet prefers to be known simply as a servant of God. Corollary chapters on the science of the spoken Word were dictated by the emissary of Jesus Christ in the Aquarian age, the "seventh angel" Saint Germain, and by the devout Saint Thomas More, devotee of the will of God in Christ who identifies himself to his chelas as the Ascended Master El Morya.

O gentle heart, the message of this book will change your life as you become a living prayer, for you already are God's very own meditation on Love.

PRAYER AND MEDITATION

JESUS AND KUTHUMI

DICTATED
TO THE MESSENGERS
MARK AND ELIZABETH PROPHET

Prayer and Meditation

Published by
SUMMIT UNIVERSITY PRESS

LIBRARY OF CONGRESS CATALOG CARD NUMBER: 76-28086

INTERNATIONAL STANDARD BOOK NUMBER: 0-916766-19-5

This book is set in 11 point Paladium with 1 point lead.

Printed in the United States of America

First Printing 1978. Second Printing 1979. Third Printing 1983
Fourth Printing 1984. Fifth Printing 1986

SUMMIT UNIVERSITY 🌙 PRESS®
LOS ANGELES

Cover painting, *Poet Seated in a Garden*, courtesy of the
Museum of Fine Arts, Boston, Massachusetts

Contents

II
The Way of Meditation
by Kuthumi

III
The Way of the Science of the Spoken Word
by Saint Germain and El Morya

IV
*The Way of the Individualization
of the God Flame
by the Messengers*

"There is a time and a place for quiet meditation, a time and a place for prayer, a time and a place for decrees." The three form a trinity of power, wisdom, and love—God the Father, God the Son, and God the Holy Spirit experienced within the temple of your being.

In the power of the spoken Word, behold how the Creator first framed the universe with the fiat "Let there be light!" In meditation, perceive the quickening of wisdom as the 'wise dominion' of the Christ mind. In prayer, let the love of the Holy Spirit become in you the integrating principle of life. When you have the trinity in this interchange, in this integration with God, your communion will work with the mathematics of the cosmos.

I

The Way of Prayer

by Jesus Christ

1

Unbroken Communion

Beloved Who Would Walk
on the Great White Way,

Unceasing communion—how laudable! how joyous! What shall I say to amplify the concept of never-ending contact? The world mind seeks to palliate through diverse and questionable measures, whereas the reality of God is best known by unbroken communion.

When Adam wandered in the Garden, communion was lost; and God said unto him, "Adam, where art thou?"[1] The infinite love of the Creator for each son of his heart continues even through the span of prodigality. All of life is rendered infinitely more grand when beheld through God's eye of light. He who extends consciousness as a pure stream of everlasting hope unto God is never soiled or damaged by a release of mortally misqualified substance.

My own, know that all substance is God; but as to the pure all things are pure, so to the unbelieving is nothing pure.[2] Those upon whom I am raying my love may not accept it in equal measure. The unbeliever may cast it aside, the skeptic question it, the dilettante vacillate from ecstasy to despair; but the cause of such reactions cannot be assigned unto the purity of my mind, derived as it is from the eternal Source, nor to the divine intent which heaven seeks to bring to full bloom through individual manifestation.

Each monadic expression, each soul, manifests yet another facet of evolutionary progress.

If evolution can be seen in the physical plane, it is even more readily discerned in the spiritual octaves and in the evolving soul where individuality draws down from heavenly heights the vestments of pure reality which remain forever unchanged.

The state of the world and of man changeth from glory unto glory, and the gathering storm of karmic encompassment shelters man not with comfort.[3] Comfort is found in the progressive acceptance of universal values, and thus men must strive to throw off those disquieting attitudes of self which veil the face of the universal Christ. If there be glory, it is for all to share; and truly there are none so blind as they who will not see.

Organizational loyalty, when practiced in good faith, is a divine attribute; but when sustained in bad faith, it is unjustifiable. Those who seek to save their lives may well lose them, but all who let flow of the native stream of God's own consciousness and infinite love through the aperture of self become as radiating points of light in time and space. These shed that eternal light upon the passing scene of mortal creation and find thereby their eternal home in the realities of heaven which are our portion.

Mindful of present world distress which, regardless of the causes and karmic roots, needs healing and transmutation, I AM come to blaze the light of God's undying reality unto all! The way of the Christ must be made known, and that way is total communion. Through ignorance men have sought to exclude their God while seeking happiness in the world. Through unbroken communion, the life experience of my final embodiment in Galilee and Nazareth can become the forte of every God-realized man.

I seek then, in response to the heart-calls of mankind, to shatter the dream that is filled with illusions, to destroy the myth that total communion is sacrificial, and to teach the way of that communion as I know it. In this statement I have begun an effort of world service to promote out of the bonds of unbroken communion a new exaltation and fount of service that, if carried out, will speedily shorten the days of men's cup of bitterness and lower into manifestation the City of God among men.

Let brotherhood increase and the light of understanding prevent hatred! For my way, the way of God, is the way of peace; and the sword of the Spirit cleaves asunder the curtain of the night and more clearly reveals that hope, eternal hope, is the nature of God. Hope can alter the unthinkable and brazen contempt of this wayward generation until the regeneration of the Son of God comes full cycle. And divine blessings in ever-increasing tempo shall magnify the light that shines behind the span of the years and the farthest reaches of space.

In gratitude for the unbroken chain of communion with the eternal Father, I remain your elder brother,

Jesus

2

Unceasing Prayer

Beloved Seekers for Wisdom,

Think on my words, "He who seeks to save his life shall lose it."[1] When you ponder the thought of unceasing prayer, consider those who fear to turn their consciousness to God lest they should miss something going on in the world around them. These seek to save their lives by involvement in the changing outer world. Those who lose (loose) their lives for my sake, by entering into the same communion with the Father which I did, truly find their life again; for only as God can live in man who exists in very being itself, life itself, does man really possess eternal life.

There is no selfishness in the Father, but only the buoyant desire to raise each lifestream into cosmic dimension. To do this before the disciple is prepared to carry the attendant responsibility could unbalance and even destroy the developing consciousness. The chalice of individuality must expand its own capacity and strength through divine grace in order that one's portion of Infinity will not overflow the banks of the chaliced cup.

Blessed ones, it is unnecessary for you to strain or to struggle in order to achieve communion with God. He is not far from you; and as near as heartbeat or thought, he can flood you with a surge of his renewing strength. Each night when you enjoy restful sleep, you experience a recharging of your blessed bodies and minds with the purity of divine energy. The extroversion of human thought and its expenditure upon myriad trivia through the day take you away from the strength of your Source. Because your energy is then depleted and its levels have fallen, you do need to renovate your consciousness, which has passed through the turmoil of a busy day.

How frequently I found during my own mission that by going up into the mountains to pray, getting away from the madding crowd, or curling up in one end of a ship, I was able to renew my strength and perform a greater ministry of service and healing.[2] All who would follow in my footsteps must understand that unless they are able to contact the great Source of life and continually renew their strength, their mission will not be carried forth in the manner desired by God. You cannot, as you say, "burn the candle at both ends" and expect it to last. Yet when it is needed, there is a limitless flow of divine strength that can be acquired as you learn to use the charging methods of divine prayer during the busiest time of the day.

Some of you are aware of the fact that the prince of this world[3] will often create a division in your mind by arranging two or more control points which clamor for your attention at the same time. In the rapid switching back and forth of your attention, your energy level drops dangerously; and when it is extremely low, that is just when the forces of negation rush in to trigger a sudden burst of anger or discouragement.[4]

This is an entirely different situation from the natural two-way flow of consciousness that can be achieved through holy communion with God right while you carry on your activities in the world. In the former case, the attention is being jockeyed back and forth between centers of interest. In the latter, your attention is moving from the world to God and from God to the world.

You need have no fear or distress that unceasing communion will disturb the efficiency of your tasks. I can truly tell you from experience that even when you are involved in difficult matters, if you carry your attention upward toward the Father and fear not the flow of his attention upon you, you can actually bathe the disquieted energies in your world with the harmony of God. And when your attention returns back into the world of form, it will no longer manifest the inharmony and imperfection that it formerly did.

Many people fear to take to God those distressing problems which involve their own personal guilt, whereas others, working in the opposite direction, seem to almost enjoy telling God how very unworthy they are. We would clarify for the benefit of all. Insofar as impure acts and thoughts go, bringing them to God for purification is in a very real sense bringing your iniquities to heaven for judgment ahead of time, thus removing from the karmic record, in many cases, the need for future recompense. "Some men's sins are open beforehand, going before to judgment; and some men they follow after."[5]

As a mother comforts a sobbing child, so

God can and does quiet the restless energies that you seem unable to govern. When you keep your problems to yourself, as though they could thus be hidden from his eye, often they are only intensified and your distress increases rather than lessens. In the matter of those who tell God how unworthy they are and appear to revel in so doing, this in most cases is the overriding of a rebellious entity or discarnate which manipulates their feelings to no good end.

You know, precious ones, the evil spirits that have lived in the world in the past and who are now out of the body, together with those possessing entities that attach themselves to individuals because they love darkness rather than light,[6] enjoy performing acts which they suspect might give distress to the Creator of the universe. This attitude is difficult for many to understand; but like that psychological trait known as masochism or self-abuse, the attempt of these spirits to flagellate the Deity by acclaiming their own dire condition actually feeds their egos and is intended to make those whom they control enjoy being sinners.

When the sincere disciple brings to the Father *all* of his energy for purification, God is truly able to wash and to regenerate with his love and attention the developing son and bring him to maturity. In cases where extreme perversions have been practiced, it will be necessary that the individual make application for forgiveness with deep sincerity and follow the injunction "Go, and sin no more."[7] Those in the latter category must of necessity strive until they have won a relative state of victory over the outer condition and understand that the demons of ego and rebellion must be put down.

There is a law involved here that states that man is accountable for that which he creates. Those who have created or harbored a rebellious spirit must themselves bring it under control and then approach God with humility that they, too, may be received and their energies purified. There is never any question whatsoever concerning the will of God to receive the prodigal son[8] back to his heart. Therefore, no one should make unworthiness an excuse for not engaging in holy prayer. The worthy need to progress and the unworthy to disentangle themselves from the enchantments of the world.

More things are indeed wrought by prayer than the world dreams of.[9] Yet ordinary prayer, strenuously engaged in, that cries out for emergency help in time of need is not to be compared with that steadfast outreach for God that understands communion as a most fortunate means to the end of personal freedom.

In memory of our Father's everlasting love for all, I remain

Jesus

3

Holy Prayer

To All Who Seek
the Resurrection:

"Thou wilt not leave my soul in hell nor suffer thine Holy One to see corruption."[1] With these words from the Psalmist, I cast out all fear of death as an unnatural process and I demonstrated for all time to all men that the way of the resurrection is the way of God living in man. Truly, he that believeth in me, though he were dead, yet shall he live;[2] for the way I know, and it is the way of abundant life.

Fear of birth could well be more justifiable than fear of death, for the rest and surcease from pain that comes to individuals who have lived a rich and full life of service to mankind is more to be desired than the pain that accompanies one's entrance into the world of form. Nicodemus queried, "Can a man, when he is old, enter once again into his mother's womb?"[3] Indeed, the simplicity of the divine plan of renewing life, either through reembodiment or the victory of overcoming mastery culminating in the ascension, is a very marvelous answer to the problems involved in the creation of individual man.

Immortal life can be retained only by the Godly. Those who acknowledge the presence of God in their lives live according to his principles, committing themselves unto God, as Daniel did in days of old, through continuous communion.[4] If I seem to pluck one note [that of unbroken

communion], it is because that note is truly the
door. To be a friend of God, you must commune
with him. To love the Father, you must know
him.

Talking to God means that your energy goes
back to the Source from whence it came, and the
Source will not refuse to answer you. It is when
men, full of fear and doubt and human criticism,
slink back into the fading image of their own
egos and in full retreat abandon the very plans
that would give them immortal life that one
could say, "Heaven weeps." For it is not the will
of God that any should perish. As has been said
of old, "My soul hath no pleasure in the death of
the wicked."[5]

> The abundant life is the natural life;
> It is the life of sun and wind,
> Of sea and earth and sky,
> Of minerals and moving vitality.
>
> God speaks through nature to man
> And he speaks through song;
> He speaks through inspiration
> And he speaks all day long.
>
> There is no end to inspiration;
> It is the firing of the spark.
> There is no end to consecration;
> 'Tis light ascending in the dark.
>
> I AM the flame of resurrection,
> The power that frees in nature's bower;
> I AM the flame of resurrection,
> Raising consciousness each hour.

To be a God (and not a clod),
True faith in plan must all expand;
To walk the pathway we have trod
The Holy Spirit now demands.

I come to give abundant life!
The treasure of thy heart is where
The human monad ceases strife
And reaches up in holy prayer.

Prayer is a ladder to God, but it is a ladder of thought that at times ceases to think and engages only in perception. The safeguards of holy prayer are love and the desire to bless, forgiveness and the will to express abundant beauty everywhere.

The chaste ideas of the Christ mind are not to be discounted or compared with those of the world mind. And those who have sought to achieve true culture need never fear the expansion of divine attunement. Neither fanaticism, insanity, nor unnatural states of mind exist in the mind of the Infinite. Oppressive mental conditions are always the result of wrong thinking and identification with the dregs of the world's thoughts.

Thus, in advocating holy prayer, we warn concerning the human tendency, after one has risen to great heights, to seek mortal comfort through a rapid descent to degrading lows. There is no need to plead with God in order to keep one's spirit in a state of truly listening grace. Rather, each soul should understand that the upward swing of the pendulum may seem to require balance in the opposite direction because it expands toward infinite heights which perhaps the fledgling soul cannot sustain; nevertheless, true balance need never be sought in extremes of unhappiness or involvement with the world.

There are certain "stops" for which one may ask when in communion with God, certain protections of one's own spiritual momentum which can and should be sought after. Frequently, those who are not given this instruction weary of well doing; and often not only do they undo all the good that they have done, but they actually put themselves momentarily backward. Sometimes the excuse that is offered by those who lack the courage to press forward is that they do not wish to go upward, for then they will have farther to fall.

There is no foundation to this theory, for those who understand the law of being are able to govern their own acts and intents even as God wishes them to do. Those at inner levels of consciousness who are for you, those who pray with you when you go up out of the mortal dimensions, are many. And if you ask them, they will help you in your descent, when for a time outer pressures may make certain demands upon your attention.

But I AM come that men may have life more abundantly;[6] and the life of more abundant prayer, of more glorious attunement, is a means to a beautiful end. Cosmic cycles are spiral segments of joy that is rising. They produce not only the purification of thought, but also the imbuement of mankind with the power from on high that enables them to sustain a momentum of beautiful example among men.

Mankind need the example of beautiful souls whose faith will help them to overcome through communion with God. One of the pitfalls that must be guarded against is the tendency on the part of men who do have divine experiences and do achieve attunement with God to become overly confident until they fall into the temptation of exalting themselves over their supposedly "lesser" brothers. This is why exhortation for the unworthy and those who are unprincipled in life is so often entered into by the masters of wisdom.

We pray for those who despitefully use us,[7] knowing that in due course of time the law will require of them a recompense for the energy that is gainfully used to puff up the ego. Thus, by seeking to save that which is lost and raising that which has fallen, we perform the work of Christ, of the illuminator, of the divine Mediator, and of the intensifier, the Holy Spirit.

Now I would like you to gaze upon the word *intensifier;* for it relates to the phrase "intended fire," and this is the fire that shall try every man's work.[8] It is the divine fire that falls upon the altar where transmutation and change are sought and wrought.

Prayer without ceasing[9] is the key to a release of radiant streams of God-energy that focus in the chalice of your being. The garnering of this energy will in time make the son to become one with the Father, for these energies are powerful and they are life. They are abundant, and they do perform within you that which mere mortal wishing can never do.

To seek to generate mortal illusion is an

unworthy act, but to seek for the regeneration of God in you is the means of overcoming the world. Again I say, pray without ceasing for your victory and for the victory of all mankind.

Radiantly in the light, I AM

Jesus the Christ

4

The Light of Prayer

Beloved Brethren of the Light,

The light of prayer, the light of communion with our Father, surges through all things. Nature is infused, man is infused, mind is infused with this beautiful light that serves as the communicator between man and God. The chasms of shadow are nothing, for the light echoes and reechoes across the widest gap. Here metaphor is reality; for the visible things of the world fade away as the invisible becomes the visible, and man through prayer sees all things bathed in a sea of luminous light-substance.

To develop this sense of all-knowing serenity is to develop the state of an untouchable being, of one who cannot be affected by outer conditions or mortal ups and downs. The light of God that never fails, beloved, awaits your call—to answer when you call and to serve your needs. The light is your obedient servant sent forth by God; for of a truth, he that would be greatest among you must be the greatest servant, and our Father is the greatest servant of all.[1]

As the beloved Son, you must recognize that your mortal role is played out upon the passing scene that leads you onward to the dawn of reality in yourself. Reality is not an outer, transient thing. Reality is the wings of the Spirit that lift mankind to a sense of omnipresence and beauty where no shadow is, but only the pulsation of the great light of God's reality.

How very foolish it is for men to suppose that their reality is wedded to mortal conditions, to think that the possessions of life can in any way lend more than passing enchantment to the scene! Let all understand, then, that the Son, beloved of the Father, is also he who loveth all things free. To be free is to breathe the Holy Spirit into the fountain of light within your heart that changes the very condition of the blood itself into liquid light and prepares you to exchange your outer garments for immortal vestments.

There is no need to fear the death of the outer man, but that the soul may be swallowed up by the vicissitudes of natural experience to the place where the divine flame that pulsates and rises within is extinguished through neglect.[2] When a bushel of outer things surrounds mankind's consciousness and leads him astray from oneness and a sense of the nearness of his own God Presence, he finds that he can lose his way.

I AM the way, and true being is the way. There is no division in true existence; therefore, there cannot be two ways. There is only one way; and that way is the indivisibility of the Spirit that has of itself created many droplets of manifestation, but all of the same Spirit. Those of you who, with me, would inherit the kingdom of God must understand, even in your outer minds, that no outer condition has any power to alter the immortal God flame blazing on the altar of your heart.

Consciousness is also possessed of a heart. The question as to whether that heart is seated in the physical heart or elsewhere in your four lower bodies, in your Holy Christ Self or in the heart of your Divine Presence, is not nearly as important as the fact that you are able to tune in with the God consciousness that is in every cell of your body and the Great Central Sun Presence of yourself, your own beloved mighty I AM Presence.

For the sense of being "I AM THAT I AM" is one, and there is no division whatsoever in this conception. There may be a multiplicity of manifestation and each one may have an assignment of specific wonder to externalize, but the beauty of the Eternal is not a passing condition. It is a permanent one. And the joy that fills the soul that is imbued with this concept is illimitable light.

Now as the dawn of holy prayer, bridging the chasm between one point and another, radiates its precious light into the consciousness of men, it speaks of the mission that seems to be impossible to those who are wedded to mortal things. This is the mission that is fulfilled when the overriding power of the Presence takes command of an individual's world and asserts its Christ-dominion as never before. Until the door is opened that leads to eternal life, men linger without and they see not the glory that is behind the portal. And until they open that door by consciously willing themselves free to be that which God created them to be, they can never know the beauty and glory that is their own. But it was so intended, for every lifestream was given the glorious mantle of ever-present perfection as an original part of the divine plan.

Lost in the descent, as man falls away from

reality into the dream of mortality, perfection seems but a dim light, half alive and questionable in the main. This is a great pity, men say, and it is so; but when men understand that I AM come that they might have light, and that more abundantly, they will also see that a rose known by any other name smells just as sweet.[3] And although men have different names for the same condition, the selfsame Spirit worketh in all to produce the miracle of communion.

I cannot under any condition fail to point out to all that communion is the full measure of salvation to every living soul; for unless man have communication with the pristine First Cause, the creative fount of divine energy and will, he may indeed lose his way in the folds of shadowed substance. But we seek for all deliverance through communion and to reinforce in all a new and living concept, that in his flesh man may see his flesh as the doorway into the Eternal. ("Yet in my flesh shall I see God.")[4]

The blessed Spirit that animates form and provides the life-energy for each day's service cannot itself be harmed by any outer condition; but the soul, in its plasticity of recording the records of living, may have scars which are best removed by application to the immortal Spirit of divine reality. God wipes away all tears from man's eyes[5] and serenely imposes the radiance of himself as a robe of righteousness over the dusty garments men have worn. The radiance of the light energy in those divine robes purifies the undergarment, and all things are penetrated by the radiance of the divine.

Have faith, keep faith, and let it mount up;

for the Brotherhood Eternal is working and
serving the causes supernal. The beauty of the
supernatural is actually in the natural manifestation, for the habitat of God is in the heaven of
man within you right where you are.

> Unfold the plan!
> See the star of present,
> Ever-present opportunity
> Gleaming from afar
> So nigh,
> Plummeting through the sky
> As hope,
> Resurrecting faith and action,
> Filling space with dreams
> Fulfilling God's will!
>
> Lo, I come—
> Still, serene,
> Pure and clean,
> To be and see
> The victory
> Of all and everyone
> That's free!

Your elder brother and gracious example,
under the wings of the eternal Father, Saviour of
each and all, I AM and remain

Jesus the Christ

5

Prayer as Communication
with Purpose

To All Who Seek
to Know God:

My love enfolds you all. The divine life is abundant, and prayer makes it possible of realization; but prayer must be regarded as communication, and communication with purpose. The world hungers for purity and lingers in guilt. 'Tis guilt that decries effort and, by creating a sense of unrighteousness and unworthiness in men, causes them to seek to hide from the Eternal Face.

Once the love of God is rightly understood by any man in any state whatsoever and he responds as prodigal son desiring to see and behold reality, reality cannot be denied unto him. God will come, and he will move in the mysterious ways of a spiritual being and a master of life to raise the individual soul into the ascended state.

Down the centuries, Christian palliatives have reduced the effectiveness of my Palestinian mission in the world of form by robbing of their import those concepts that are most important and stressing conditions which are a part of the lesser mysteries of God. For example, the via dolorosa, the sorrowful way, has been over-emphasized and the suffering which I supposedly experienced is pointed out to mankind as a thorny road which they may expect to follow to their freedom.

Yet my words so clearly spoken to the weeping women of Jerusalem, "Weep not for me, ye daughters of Jerusalem, but weep for yourselves

and for your children," seem to have been forgotten.[1] "The way ye know" is now the way
known by the few, yet the many regard themselves as "the elect." To make your calling and
election sure, you must commune with Reality;
you must commune with humility and you must
commune with absolute sincerity.[2]

Out of the bane of uncertainty, men excuse
themselves from communion and they pursue
those enervating pleasures of the world which
bring them to discouragement and doubt. Faith
requires the fuel of fervent effort and fervent
communion. Each time an individual feels the
fires of reality dying down within the furnace of
self, he must once again renew his covenant with
God and seek to raise those fires to a place where
the throb and pulsation of that inward reality
can be felt and known within one's own flesh and
the flesh of true identity.

Men identify with themselves outwardly,
with their person, and cease altogether the
recognition of the heavenly image.

> The heavenly image is the thought
> God used as blueprint plan,
> As architectural demand upon the universe
> To fabricate and design
> A perfect man, a holy sign,
> Symbol of the flame encased in form,
> The dual Paraclete reborn.
> As Holy Spirit manifest in men,
> This is the visit of our God again
> To world that 'waits the dawn.

O beloved ones, in this hour of world peril
when the throb of Armageddon is heard as

violence in the streets and as fear coming to
many hearts, there is a need in America and in
the world to renew the diligent application of
prayer that burned on Quaker's hearth and in
patriot's home. There, love was a glowing fire
that sought itself to nourish a nation and cause
this great land to expand wholesomely, teaching
the young courtesy and grace and the art of
loving one another.

Modern methods do not surpass the old.
The latter are enhanced by scientific achievement
and a richer measure of technological embellish-
ment. If such elements of progress were used for
the furtherance of the kingdom of God upon
earth today and to teach the law as we intend it
to be taught, it would be truly to place the
kingdom within the grasp of men. But in this
hour when communication has become so
readily possible on a larger scale, the voices of
the night are heard and the voices of the day are
stilled; they are lost in the blare and tumult of the
film makers and commercial vested interests and
in the hammer of religious dogma.

Now a thrust for a purpose must be made
into the world and the kingdom of God be
brought very close to men! I am come again in
this age to communicate with a larger body of
men upon the planet than has inhabited it for
many a year. Men are rich and increased with
goods, but they do not understand that the
passing moment they have is but an opportunity
for bringing about increased good. And how essential is the increased good of imparting communication from the ageless fount of wisdom to
a dying youth that with heavy heart seeks to cast

away the carnal mold that he witnesses!

Today, we of hierarchy, mindful of the prayers rising unto Deity for assistance to the world in her hour of need, stress that with God-speed valiant assistance must come forth to men; and the work that The Summit Lighthouse seeks to do must be implemented, for it is a service in which all can unite. Hierarchy seeks not to build through this means a mere secular tower rising unto the skies, but to teach in this day the lost art of communion with God to honor the Deity, that the family of nations may perchance avoid the awful debacle toward which it is headed.

In the days of the Tower of Babel,[3] the Great Karmic Board and heavenly hosts did cause to be issued the edict that confused the people's speech and drove them into separate bands in order that the awful contagion of unrighteousness might be stopped. Today the world has restored outer communication, but it is swiftly losing every vestige of the culture of the immortals.

The Great White Brotherhood, in a desperate attempt to stop this headlong debasement of the sons of God and children of the light upon the planet, is calling to all who will hear my voice and summoning the council of the elect from the four corners of the earth to a vigil of such holy prayer as has never before been raised as sweet incense to the throne of grace.

All men, then, must learn to recognize that in the span of the few short years and smothering dogmas to which they are exposed, they do not learn all of the manifold mysteries of God that are taught in the schools and archives of light. Heaven has become a nebulous name to many, and God a myth. Both are real, tangible, and powerful.

Without heaven and heaven's God, life would lack purpose and meaning; for God framed the world with holy wisdom and gave to man free will in order that, like Prometheus unbound, he might create reality within himself and achieve his own Godhood. This glorious concept has been cast aside by delusion and by the contagion of error so that men today are but a shadow of their former selves and the light is nearly gone out. Yet the light lives and the light is abundant! The light is real and prayer and communication are the requirements of the day.

Your beloved Saint Germain wrote in *Macbeth*, "Out, damned spot! out, I say!"[4] Let us then decree to "out" the darkness in all men and to radiate the light of love to one another, no matter what men may think or do! Above all, let us decree that each individual soul, expressing the greatness of the Divine Self, may learn the precious art of weaving the golden flow of the shuttle of attention between himself and his God, between the son and the Father, between darkness and light. Thus shall light inhabit darkness and dispel it and bring to all the wedding garments of eternal purpose that cause the holy spiritual Bride of the Church to say, "Behold, the Bridegroom cometh!"[5]

For the radiant purposes of God's will in all, I remain and I AM

Jesus the Christ

6

Universal Prayer

To All Who Aspire
to Continual Prayer:

The term "Our Father" signifies mutuality and sharing. The perfect life descending from God into the manifestation of self has been strained by mortal misqualification of its original intent and purity. But the desecrations and stains, created in ignorance, are blotted out by the effulgence of the greater light of the indwelling Christ.

No pagan or sacrificial act is involved when the son of God cast in the prodigal mold seeks to be free. It is the universal Christ, the everlasting light of the eternal Father that raiseth all upon the ladder of progressive reality until the world of heaven engulfs the individual seeker for unity.

Myriad doctrines, dogmas, and entrenched concepts have drained mankind of strength and made him a victim of satanic myth. The father of lies has spun many an idle dream and used it as a psychic net to divide and conquer large blocks of individuals in the religious community.[1] Often the seeker for truth is made merchandise of and the very hunger in his soul for righteousness causes him, in fanatical zeal, to disclaim his own birthright and to proclaim as truth the teachings of the synagogue of Satan.[2]

The reality of the Christ is the leaven of truth that serves in the world of the individual to elevate his consciousness toward service in the

light. That which would divide the body of God
on earth, that which would classify certain
believers as "evil," that which would deny
fellowship to them as brethren and spread the
poison of gossip and deceit is always of malicious
intent—if not in the person of the purveyor of
such teachings, then in the spirit that controls the
person.

Those who desire Christ-unity in the family
of religious seekers understand that Antichrist
has already come and is in the world.[3] My prayer
"Father, make them one even as we are one" is
not intended to promulgate a unity of op-
positional doctrines, but to prevail upon men to
behold in childlike simplicity that God is one.[4]
Simply put, this means that Good is one, and
that oneness is Good. Naturally, deceit and error
cannot be united with goodness, but then deceit
and error have no part of God or of his teaching.
These are created by the powers of darkness as
confusing elements which lead men astray and
divide hearts from hearts.

The body of Christ on earth can best be activated in universal harmony as men cease to consider the mandates of dogma as the primary requirement in determining "Who is my brother?"
Rather let men see all men as brothers essen-
tially—that is, in essence, in divine intent—and
in an orderly progression toward Christly acceptance of one another as joint-heirs of the
kingdom.[5]

When men accept the reality of the living
Christ for themselves as individuals, they realize that the ascension in the light is a progressive achievement that they themselves will one

day experience—as individuals. To be lifted
out of the dregs and doldrums of mortal thought
and feeling, from all sense oppression and
unrighteousness, into the electronic throb of
the universal heart, with its attendant restora-
tion of man's total communicative facilities, is
to receive a blessing of incomparable glory.
To this great measure of God-reality, to this res-
toration of individuality, to communication with
the Holy of Holies, we are dedicated for every
man.

The broad road will narrow, and the narrow
road that leadeth to eternal life will expand as
man passes through the portals of succeeding
tests into the trackless dimensions of the Infinite.
The seeker has found! No longer pinned to the
blight of continuous questioning and probing, he
now beholds reality, the Invisible made visible.
By holy prayer all men can attain both oneness
with God and the poignant reunion of souls who
have long been severed from one another by the
betrayal of negative karma. The breaches will be
healed, the fruit of man's labors will be made
tangible and real, and the kingdom of God will
be seen as possible of attainment by those who
have underestimated the potential of life that is
within them.

What a boon to universal manifestation is to
be found in universal prayer!

> 'Tis a hymn
> That, humming lightly,
> Penetrates the air—
> A wave of light,
> Manifesting everywhere.

Sun glow and sun fire,
Hope's radiant desire—
Manchild manifesting
Spiritual Intensifier.

I AM THAT I AM—so pure,
Imbued with cosmic power.
I shall endure
All assailing, flailing
Outer things,
By consecration now within
Expand my wings.
I, too, shall win—
I shall rise!
No more by carnal bound,
My rising soul hears
The universal sound.

Where God is, there I AM,
And everywhere's my prayer.
'Tis fragrance's evolving spin
That shapes my destiny through prayer.
Communication with the One,
Our Father dear,
Thou radiance of the Central Sun,
Appear!
By light I glow,
Thy word I hear:
Beloved Son, through love
Cast out all fear!
Thy work is mine;
To thee I say, "Well done!"
For faith and hope
And charity are one;
Attainment comes as seed of God
Right here within thyself.

Expand and know the fullness
Of the inner light that glows
To teach, to counsel, to enfold!
I AM the cosmic law
Of elder race of old
That, shining down
The pathway of the years,
Has sought to guide,
To wipe away all human tears,
To show the power of the inner light,
The inner faith, the inner might,
To shape and reshape the course of men,
To cause the holy kingdom
To be born again in men.

"Come then, let us reason together," saith God:
"My law of love and truth is heaven's rod.
I stretch it forth in barren wilderness.
I make the hopeful blossoms to confess
The Lord is God."
He will bestow the wonders
Of communion to mankind below.
He'll raise the earth
And every man that's here
And let the cosmic universal Christ appear.

Why will ye tarry, blessed ones?
Why will ye delay as you pass this way?
It is a golden opportunity
Restoring great sincerity
And cosmic purpose old,
Restoring communication
With the God of old
Who maketh all things new
And swiftly bringeth into view
The greater light.

Blessed ones, join with me in the prayer of faith that all men may be one, even as God is one. Join with me in faith that true integration with Eternal Law will come to every man. In truth this is the master plan.

Abundantly, in the never failing response of universal prayer by every cosmic being, your

Jesus the Christ

7

Continual Prayer

To All Who Seek
Greater Communion:

I consider true prayer to be a cornucopia, a cylinder of abundant blessings. The showering of these blessings may require a bit of shaking of the bower, as the receiving cup of the disciple is lifted upward in holy anticipation. Between the dark and the daylight—the dark of unmanifest substance and the daylight of manifestation—there is at times a slip of needless dissipation. Excess anticipation of self-good without self-surrender drains spiritual treasure and prevents manifestation.

Childlike trust should rise to become man-like sensibility where, through the process of natural development, the life of the individual is seen as an opportunity to become Godlike. The man who does for himself what others expect God to do for them, according to the best understanding he has and the limit of his personal capacities, will soon find flowing through his consciousness a unit of transcendent life which I call the abundant life.

When I brake the bread before the five thousand, the one loaf easily became the many; for all substance is one and all power is one.[1] When universal good is the motivating principle and selfishness is cast down through the individual's desire to serve the perfection of life, he is often granted a release of unparalleled strength—the strength of the Divine, the abundance of the

Divine, the purity of God, the wisdom of God, and the love of God.

The nature of the Father is within the Son. It is within ye all, now and always. When you reach up hands of seeking faith and allow the unbroken prayer of steadfast purpose to act, you are opening the door to that perfect understanding that transcends all mortal sense of limitation.

Some say: "Why need I read? Why must I consider these things?" Precious ones, as above, so below. Man's sense of individuality and his perception in the world of form have been builded through the centuries as the soul, outwardly perceiving substance, fashioned its own inward sense of substance and circumstance. It is just as necessary in dealing with spiritual matters for the individual to program himself, to orient himself, to prepare himself through cosmic study to grasp universal principles as it is for him to grasp external ones.

A release such as I am giving in my series on continual prayer is invaluable to the aspirant; for it conveys thought matrices calculated to develop in each one who studies an inward approval of the consciousness of the universal Creator, our heavenly Father. Most unfortunate is it that the same words of life which I speak are often spoken by laymen, ministers, and teachers who claim to be of the eternal craft of builders and are not. Through much hearing, the ears of men have waxed dull;[2] and there is a tendency to compare the fruits of other men's labors with their words. This brings the individual to a sense of judgment where he spends too much of his time in judging the lives of others and not enough

time in communion with God whereby he seeks
to erase the results of negative assaults upon his
own soul. Thus men often become critics whose
criticism denies the fruit of progress to themselves.

We seek then to show forth the fact that no
matter how many spiritual words may be spoken
by men in surface utterance, using ideas or
expressions similar to our own, unless the Spirit
lives behind the Word, the flesh is as grass and
continues so to be. The conveyance which has
been cited as "the laying on of hands," or the
transfer of the Spirit, must be made through the
universal life-principle whereby one actually
contacts God.[3]

God lives, the Father lives, and he lives in
you. But you must evoke him by continual
prayer until the strands of discord that bind you
to the world are severed for all time, until the
opaquing clouds of mortal densities are blown
away by the wind of the Holy Spirit, until the
sun shining in his strength is seen by you and
drawn down into the chalice cup as the fire of life
unto regeneration.[4] Unless this be done, you
cannot drink of the cup of which I drink or
partake of the baptism with which I am baptized;[5] for there is but one Holy Spirit, and he
manifests to all the knowledge of the Father. You
are baptized into one body.[6] There is but one
Great White Brotherhood of light; and all souls
aspiring to it, who enter into it, enter into the
One.

My reason for reiterating these facts in this
discourse on prayer is that there has been formed
down through the ages a pseudocult of religious

seekers who would build a hedge around themselves, claiming a sovereign superiority in dogma, in teaching, and in possessing the things of God. This attitude forestalls the manifestation of reality and creates inharmony between peoples. Our will, as God's will, is one; it is to create from the one life the manifestation of the manifold and to create from the many the one. It is not in the mere acceptance of the pressure of socially or religiously acceptable ideas that men become wise. Progress is obtained outside of sect and order, yet to deny that it exists within sect and order is to deny that God has worked with individuals and societies down through the ages.

You must learn to become the arbiter of your own destiny, not by denial and severance, not by separation in all cases, but through understanding that the advent of the Eternal moves through societies and orders, through organizations and peoples, manifesting for a season in this or that order and then, in the interest of progress, forming a new order of the ages. We must have access to men's consciousness in order to bring forth new ideas, yet it must be clear that the new ideas are also the old truths that have always lived in the universe.

It is man himself who, through misunderstanding and a false, exalted sense of his own worth, has cast stones of stumbling[7] in his brother's pathway. That these may be removed is our prayer. Yet it is too much to expect that everyone will understand our effort, our existence, and our ability to communicate with mankind in this day as in former times.

I live now even as I lived then, and my life is

continual, as is your own. To have and to hold this sense is to keep forever the unbroken communion with God that pushes back the clouds of unknowing and transfers into all outer conditions the joy of the Lord that he expresses in the rose, in the soul, in the child, in man, in woman, in the birds that fly, in the wind that blows, in the gentle rain, in the dew upon the grass, in the breath of life, in the consciousness of peace, in the hope of becoming, and in the triumph of victory.

In all things God *is*. He animates all, he lives in all; yet he is unknown by many. He sings the song of the new day which comes into view as the shadow of former things passes away and all things become new.[8]

Your humble servant in the divine domain,

Jesus

8

*Prayer Offerings
of the Lord Jesus Christ*

I AM Lord's Prayer

Our Father who art in heaven,
Hallowed be thy name, I AM.
I AM thy kingdom come
I AM thy will being done
I AM on earth even as I AM in heaven
I AM giving this day daily bread to all
I AM forgiving all life this day even as
I AM also all life forgiving me
I AM leading all men away from temptation
I AM delivering all men from every evil condition
I AM the kingdom
I AM the power and
I AM the glory of God in eternal, immortal
    manifestation—
All this I AM.

Transfiguring Affirmations

I AM THAT I AM
I AM the open door which no man can shut
I AM the light which lighteth every man
   that cometh into the world
I AM the way
I AM the truth
I AM the life
I AM the resurrection
I AM the ascension in the light
I AM the fulfillment of all my needs
   and requirements of the hour
I AM abundant supply poured out upon all life
I AM perfect sight and hearing
I AM the manifest perfection of being
I AM the illimitable light of God
   made manifest everywhere
I AM the light of the holy of holies
I AM a son of God
I AM the light in the holy mountain of God

Heavenly Light

O star of eternal perfection, shine in me!
O star of eternal perfection, shine through me!
O star of radiant wonder,
Flash forth thy rays into the world!
Burn through dark sheaths of hate,
Fear, greed, and unbelief—
Tear the veil from the face of injustice—
Open the gates, and let flow
The love of the Infinite here below!
Wherever I AM, wherever I go,
Eternal Presence, let light flow!

To Doers

Communion supreme,
Ecstasy's dream—
I and my Father are one.
Communion's pure gleam,
Sweet approbation—
Every deed now well done.
Service is raising,
As life I AM praising—
Peace from the Father, the Son.
Light resurrecting,
Each one perfecting
Hears that sweet voice,
"Tis well done."

I Serve Them

Father, forgive them,
They know not what they do.
Their lives are encircled
By heavenly blue—
Thy will everlasting
Belongs unto all,
So raise them, dear Father
(don't let them fall).

The lost and confused,
Though wandering afar,
Need thy great hand
To heal every mar.
Then lift every burden,
And heal every stain;
Let all of the hopeless
Hear thee again.

O come unto me,
All ye who labor,
My rest is for you;
Each heavenly favor
I gladly do give,
So that ye may live
In life more abundant.

Where'er ye may go,
Let God work through you—
His power does flow.
There're many who need you
And what you can do,
So live for the many,
And raise up the few
Who will listen and love me,
For I AM the One—
The heavenly Father,
The heavenly Son—

My light is the light
Of the whole blessed world.
It shines right through you
As lustrous pearl,
A treasure forever,
A glimpse of the real:
May God ever seal you
In all that is real.

Hidden Unity

So low and yet so high—
So far and yet so nigh,
Blazing, blazing through the sky,
Comes my flame of peace.

Darkness fades,
Life's great waves
Engulfing to untie
Every knot of blinding bind,
Causing men to sigh.

Peace that lives
Heaven gives,
Freedom from on high,
Flames that leap
God does seek—
Hope eternal, rise!

Prayer will kindle
On the spindle,
Threading from the skies—
Communion way, love today
Descends as sweet surprise.

A Little Child

A little child shall lead them—
The eye so meek and mild—
A little child shall feed them,
Where is the little child?
Right within you
Golden man,
His flaming image flashes,
Expanding now
As son of man,
Meteoric flashes!
The way ye know,
The way to go
Reveals in sudden flashes,
That to live you must forgive
Man for sodden clashes!
Victory's gleam
Will send a stream,
Renewing each man's portion:
The dead shall rise
Unto the skies
And live in purest thought!
This life is real
And will not steal
The truth that I have brought—
My word abiding
Now is hiding
In the soul that God hath wrought.
This little child
So meek and mild
Is man whom God hath taught.

The Good Shepherd

I AM the shepherd boy,
My flock abides within my heart;
To shelter them from every ploy,
To seal God's love, I now impart
A touch of God's own hand—
All life I do command.

All power's mine,
And whosoever will, may come—
Let not the sun
Go down upon your wrath,
But walk with me the sacred path
That loves men free—
Who cannot see, as yet,
My rod and staff as needed
For the journey still ahead.

By stillest waters,
Stay and eat my bread—
I AM the living Word
In quiet places of the land,
In radiant white and purer love,
I stand—
To raise the fallen,
Helping men to understand
My burden's light.

My strong command
Will rally for the fight,
For victory o'er the earth,
Delight restoring
Sense of worth and hope:
I give new birth
By holy word I spoke—

I speak again,
"No shadowed thing shall stand
Between thee and thy God!"
For freedom in thy soul
Will free thee from the sod—
Enclosure of the mortal form
And, by descending fire,
Weave a Spirit body
To adorn thy consciousness
That lifts a song
To dearest Father of us all
And, singing all day long,
Does answer heaven's call:

I AM Good Shepherd,
One who loves thee, too,
I ask you now to bring
Unto my view
A greater vision,
Largesse of the heart;
To darkened world
New hope we must impart,

And falling mantle,
As a shooting star,
Clothe the world
So naked in distress,
That every heart
May lovingly confess,

"I need thee Lord,
Thy plan do make my own."
Let love for everyone atone
Until the veil for all
Is rent in twain;
And life, all life,
Is radiant in my name.

It Is Finished!

It is finished!
Done with this episode in strife,
I AM made one with immortal life.
Calmly I AM resurrecting my spiritual energies
From the great treasure house of immortal knowing.
The days I knew with thee, O Father,
Before the world was—the days of triumph,
When all of the thoughts of thy being
Soared over the ageless hills of cosmic memory;
Come again as I meditate upon thee.
Each day as I call forth thy memories
From the scroll of immortal love,
I AM thrilled anew.
Patterns wondrous to behold enthrall me
With the wisdom of thy creative scheme.
So fearfully and wonderfully am I made
That none can mar thy design,
None can despoil the beauty of thy holiness,
None can discourage the beating of my heart
In almost wild anticipation
Of thy fullness made manifest within me.

O great and glorious Father,
How shall a tiny bird created in hierarchical bliss
Elude thy compassionate attention?
I AM of greater value than many birds
And therefore do I know that thy loving thoughts
Reach out to me each day
To console me in seeming aloneness,
To raise my courage,
Elevate my concepts,
Exalt my character,

Flood my being with virtue and power,
Sustain thy cup of life flowing over within me,
And abide within me forever
In the nearness of thy heavenly presence.

I cannot fail,
Because I AM thyself in action everywhere.
I ride with thee
Upon the mantle of the clouds.
I walk with thee
Upon the waves and crests of water's abundance.
I move with thee
In the undulations of thy currents
Passing over the thousands of hills
    composing earth's crust.
I AM alive with thee
In each bush, flower, and blade of grass.

All nature sings in thee and me,
For we are one.
I AM alive in the hearts of the downtrodden,
Raising them up.
I AM the law exacting the truth of being
In the hearts of the proud,
Debasing the human creation therein
And spurring the search for thy reality.
I AM all things of bliss
To all people of peace.
I AM the full facility of divine grace,
The Spirit of Holiness
Releasing all hearts from bondage into unity.

It is finished!
Thy perfect creation is within me.
Immortally lovely,
It cannot be denied the blessedness of being.
Like unto thyself, it abides in the house of reality.
Nevermore to go out into profanity,
It knows only the wonders of purity and victory.
Yet there stirs within this immortal fire
A consummate pattern of mercy and compassion
Seeking to save forever that which is lost
Through wandering away
From the beauty of reality and truth.
I AM the living Christ in action evermore!

It is finished!
Death and human concepts have no power
   in my world!
I AM sealed by God-design
With the fullness of that Christ-love
That overcomes, transcends, and frees the world
By the power of the three-times-three
Until all the world is God-victorious—
Ascended in the light and free!

It is finished!
Completeness is the allness of God.
Day unto day an increase of strength, devotion,
Life, beauty, and holiness occurs within me,
Released from the fairest flower of my being,
The Christ-consecrated rose of Sharon
Unfolding its petals within my heart.
My heart is the heart of God!
My heart is the heart of the world!
My heart is the heart of Christ in healing action!
Lo, I AM with you alway, even unto the end,
When with the voice of Immortal Love
I too shall say, "It is finished!"

II

The Way
of Meditation

by Kuthumi

*Meditation
upon the Rainbow
of Light's Perfection*

Blessed Disciples
of Holy Wisdom,

The miracle of attunement is many-sided. Our beloved Jesus has emphasized continual prayer. I have been asked by the brothers of light of the Darjeeling Council to discourse on the subject of meditation. Let the words of my mouth and the meditation of my heart be acceptable in thy sight.[1]

Jesus and I desire jointly that the words and deeds that men do should be Godlike. Prayer and meditation are like twins framing the pathway to holiness and delight. Just as prayer or entreaty makes contact with God, drawing down into the world of the seeker the rays of divine intercession, so, meditation lifts up the Son of man that he may be bathed in the radiance of the Eternal.

Meditation is an aerating of the mind, a flushing-out of silt and misconception. Meditation is for purification. It is the thought of man about his Creator. The dust of the world must be blown away, the threshing floor of the heart of man swept clean. In prayer man makes intercession to God for assistance; in meditation he gives assistance to God by creating the nature of God within his own thoughts and feelings.

Many pray from the standpoint of the sinner asking forgiveness for sin. But after forgiveness what? After forgiveness for the sin must come the re-creation of the Divine Man. As man was

framed in the mortal image, so must he be
formed now in the image of the Eternal. It has
not been enough that the image of God, from its
lofty position, has been vouchsafed to every
man. The gift has not been received in manifestation.

Therefore, to meditate upon the gift is to
draw the attunement of the soul toward the harmony of God realization. If man has been a thief,
now he becomes the giver. If he has thought
evil of others, now he becomes the mediator, the
intercessor, the meditator upon their perfection
as well as upon his own, reaffirming by his acts
the mission of the Christ. The universe is a
many-stringed lute. The infinite range of its
harmonies can be enjoyed by all; but newness of
sight and of hearing, newness of education, the
schooling of the vision to transmit lofty thoughts
and to transform them that they may come
within the reach of the outstretched fingers of
man—all of this man must make his own. God
has proposed; his laws have disposed. Man has
rejected; now he must perfect.

The admonishment of your beloved Hilarion,
known unto many as Saint Paul, was "Think on
these things."[2] To meditate, then, is to let the
thoughts of God that flow into the heart rise
into the head, that the Knower may also become
the known. Meditation is an exchange of man's
imperfect thoughts about himself and his Creator
for the perfect thoughts held for him by the
Creator. Identifying now with the eternal God,
who is his Creator, the highest in his nature
becomes the joint creator of himself. Thus, in a
very real sense, as man draws the perfection of

God into his world, he becomes the arbiter of his own destiny—a co-worker in the sublime—and he becomes as God is, self-created and creating.

The creative power of the universe that emanates from the highest Source is given to the earth beneath in order that man may learn through the alchemy of meditation to change, as your beloved Gautama has indicated, the *dust* of his world into the *destiny* of the Eternal. The stars are your portion, as is the magnificent God flame within your heart. The miniature sun of illumination within is the golden pot at the end of the rainbow of light's extension into your world.

Where light is, there God is, daubing the many colors of the pure white light into a kaleidoscope resembling Joseph's coat of many colors.[3] For of a truth, just as the seamless garment[4] of the Lord Christ Jesus was white indeed, so in his embodiment as Joseph he wore the coat of many colors. The many became the one in the Christ, and out of that Christ light can be drawn forth the many colors of universal perfection.

In a like manner, those who would follow the Christ in the regeneration of the light within may meditate upon the relationship of the colors of the rainbow of light's perfection:

Blue (the first ray) is the token of faith, of promise, of constancy, of power, of strength, of the earnestness of God. It flows out of vast luminous reservoirs into sea and sky. It is Tuesday's blessing to the earth.

Yellow (the second ray) is the melding of the gold and the white as a golden radiance whose glimmer imparts illumination, the consecration of right knowledge, the service of right knowledge, the outshining of the Christ mind, and the establishment of the law of harmonious relations between all peoples and between God and all peoples. It is the ray of the sun sent to the earth on Sunday.

The aurora of the dawn, pink (the third ray), is the symbol of divine love—a love that, as floral token, floods across the plains and graces the bowers of the imagination with a garment of trailing arbutus, the scent of a pink rose. Love is joyous, buoyant, and beautiful. Through the power of love, men learn how they may impart unto others the beauty and the compassion that they have received from God. In the giving of this charity and beauty, there is no robbery, but only the fair exchange among all souls who are ennobled by the same love that God is. Monday is imbued with this creative power.

The white of purity (the fourth ray) is a stellar radiance. While composing all of the colors of the rainbow, it has its own gigantic sheath that, as a sea of liquid flame, holds before the children of men the longing to be a part of that which can never be contaminated by reason or by deceitful act. Purity—the mind of God, the nature of God, the character of God, freedom from stain, freedom from blame, the triumphant merging of the many colors into the purity of the One, whiting man toward foreverness, celebrating man's purification on the cross of white fire on Good Friday, the day of freedom when through purity man obtains his freedom from the bonds of limitation.

And what of the green (the fifth ray) imbuing all life with the perfect blend of the yellow and the blue, evidencing the faith and wisdom of God in nature and speaking of eternal newness? The green, the wearing of the green, charges man with the healthful and health-giving chlorophyll of the sun—the fire of the sun and the fire of the power to create locked in a mighty omen of healing green, restoring man to the primal nature of God. Endowed and endowing, the ray of green supplies man with every lack as it penetrates the earth on Wednesday.

The purple and the gold (the sixth ray) are the vestments that imbue man with the desire for cosmic service, emblems symbolical of the priesthood of true believers. The purple speaks of the illumined fire of the soul. This fire must assist every part of life to find reunion with its Source and with the golden law that God has dispensed to men. It is the ministration of the Christ to his disciples, of the servant who is greatest. This twofold action of God's body (purple) and his essence (gold) bathes the earth on Thursday.

When it comes to synthesizing into action the rays of love and power, the pink and the blue, there is born the radiance of the violet flame (the seventh ray). Also called the royal purple, it shows aborning within the consciousness the sense of the mantle. God has caressed and blessed the individual. Now he must wear the mantle of diplomacy, the robe of tact and of judgment. He must mediate as best he can for lesser men, for those who have not yet advanced to his level of attainment. Whether man, angel, or master, he must serve the cause of freedom, delivering men from the bondages they themselves have created. No thanks must he expect, but only the holding in grateful heart of the feeling of gratitude for more service in order that tomorrow he may give in greater measure that which he has given in lesser measure today. Saturday—the day to pause and consider the ritual of freedom.[5]

Transcendence, then, is the nature of the light; and as we draw our meditations into the light, we see that there is much to contemplate. Let us aspire! Let us lift up our heads, for our redemption draweth nigh.

From Wisdom's fount may we drink.

Lovingly,
Kuthumi

10

*Plunging into
the Ocean of God*

May Wisdom's Flame
Surround You!

Throughout the world men extol meditation as a means to self-realization—to nirvana, to the triumph of the individual in his relationship with God. Meditation takes many forms, but when it takes the form of the meditator and brings him into the fiery furnace of God's love, to the crucible of God's will, to the fount of illumination that he may drink, to the mantle of service that he may give, and to the expressing of the abundance of nature in his life which he purifies through meditation and frees from desires inordinate, then and only then can the ascended masters and the cosmic hierarchy use the individual to the fullest.

I speak of meditations which are like unto individuals who are afraid to get wet. They dangle their feet in the ocean and fearfully, momentarily, and always prepare to run from the inundating waves. Meditation, then, must be entered with a willingness to go where God goes.

We are aware of the fact that in the world today, as always, ignorant men are quick to impute to any relatively new religion the responsibility for disturbing men's minds, for "disturbing the peace." For example, if someone who is associated with a new religion has a mental or an emotional disturbance, friends, parents, and relatives may say, "He has lost his mind because of this new religion."

Every day mankind, many of whom have no religion at all, are losing their minds over matters of far less concern; and while we admit that some men have lost their minds about religion, these would probably have lost their minds about any number of things in which they might have become engaged; for the seeds of their disturbances were involved in their own karma and the record needed purification. In other cases, benign individuals have been disturbed by their own sense of struggle in searching for God. These need to learn the power of relaxation, of total commitment, and of a divine constancy that suffereth no punishing sense simply because it aspires.

Aspire to the highest, if you will, in your meditations and in your thoughts; but do not be disturbed or frustrated because any particular day does not bring to you the full fruition of that which you seek. The fruit is in the very bud of aspiration; and, given time to come full cycle, Nature will bring the fruit to your feet.

I do not say that exposure to the sun, to the air, and to good thoughts constantly obtained will not enhance your chances of bearing fruit; nor do I think that the time cannot be shortened, for it can. However, we do wish to point out that meditation carried on by sound minds can produce greater soundness of mind and healing than meditation that is carried on by unsound minds. For the benefit of all concerned, I would mention certain observations and requirements in the practice of the art of meditation.

First, one must obtain the sense of one's self. The ancient maxim "Man, know thyself"[1] is the key to the spiritualization of the self which must be known ere it can be transformed. Then one must quiet the vibratory conditions and waves of feeling and thought that lurk everywhere in the atmosphere seeking to disquiet the individual. After one has succeeded in quieting the turmoil of mind and feeling, thoughts about others, about self, about deeds one feels have been performed to one's hurt, after regrets are stilled and the mind is emptied of its negative content, it is ready then to begin the process of feeding upon the divine ideal.

What is the character of God? What is his nature? How can his nature be known? Will the knowledge of the character of God obtained from the Universal be lacking in any bookish interpretation or scholarly rendering written by saints and sages of the past? Will the individual suffer as the result of his own meditations upon God? Will he become separated in mind and heart through whatever advancement is handed to him?

Now once again the mind must be stilled; one's motive must be reexamined. Why am I meditating? I am meditating upon God that I may become Godlike. Is God aloof to the world or is he simply inaccessible? If God is aloof to the world, then of course the result of meditation would be to make the devotee also aloof, creating a spiritual snobbishness. But if God is only relatively inaccessible to the world simply because men cannot or do not reach up to him, this fact should not interfere with the orderly course of man's meditation, providing he does not try to convey to others all of the internal

loftiness and spiritual gifts of knowledge imparted to him in his meditations.

All that is received in one's private meditations is not intended to be copied down and
made into a set of academic rules to govern the
spiritual unfoldment of others. Much internal
training is given to smoothen the ruffles in one's
own nature in order that he may, in the eyes of
the heavenly Father, do one thing and one thing
alone; and that is, reflect God. That which is
required of one may not be required of another;
for as long as there are disturbances in his
receptor mechanism or scratches on the mirror-
like surface of his mind and heart, every anom-
aly, every wrinkle, will make an imperfect
picture.

Meditation, then, is to quiet the storms that
rage in the personal self, that foment maya[2] in
consciousness. It is to purify and calm the atmosphere of thought that men might realize that
all things less than divine are simply not divine
(yet men have imbued them with their own ideas
and objective realities).

Now man must recognize the Spirit of the
Lord that bloweth the wind. The Invisible must
become visible unto him. He must deal with
subtleties and cosmic innuendos. He must recognize the whisperings of the voice of God that
teach him the meaning of love—"Lord, make
me an instrument of thy peace." Man must become an instrument for all Good (all of God)
to all men; but he must perceive as God does that
he cannot always do more than to radiate his
attainment softly, imperceptibly into the
universe. To force his opinions and discoveries

upon others can put him in the position of being the target of much resentment.

The disciple who meditates upon God must learn the art of graciously identifying with God, whose mounting concerns for the world are real and tangible today as they have always been. His concern shines with the sun of his constancy; yet he feels no pang of distress or pull into the maelstrom of human discontent, the depravity of men's depredations.

Now the soul is with God. God is the sole reality of being, and reality is contacted by the disciple. What must he do with this great commodity which he has imported from the highest realms but which he cannot impart to any below, save to those who are ready? Is not his role to make himself a doorway for the greater light which he feels he cannot dispense? But is this wall of nondispensation all-engrossing? And is it true that he cannot dispense the greater light or impart it unto any?

The power of example is the strongest bond in the world that speaks of the Most High having descended to mankind. What shall I say, then, of the avatars, of the great ones who have come as mighty lights blazing through the heavens—the Christ who came teaching and preaching the good news, the Buddha who came meditating and explaining the Eightfold Path, Mohammed who came as on a fiery steed, stirring and imparting the knowledge of the law, and of the many others who have descended to the earth to do the will of God?

It is a mistake, blessed ones, to assume that one must lag behind and wait because family, friends, or neighbors do not respond to those powerful but subtle emanations of God that have always existed in the atmosphere. Meditate, then, with the idea of plunging into the ocean of God! Meditate with the idea of obtaining all that God has in store for you! Meditate with the idea of finding the Most High God if it costs all that you have and more! Go in debt for it if you must, but realize that meditation is mediation between God and man!

Your thoughts must become chalices into which God can place the truth about himself; and when that truth is known within the framework of the relative, as more and more upon earth aspire toward their ascension, they will find that removing veils is a joyous experience. We do not deny that it can be difficult, for men have often identified with the veils they have created. But now through meditation these veils will be removed one by one, and the burning power of the light will show man a new archetype of himself.

Onward and upward into the light in search of truth, I remain

Kuthumi

A Journey into the Temple Most Holy

Beloved Devotees of Reality,

The posture of man in meditation is examined. Among those who would meditate upon God are men of action and diligence as well as men of sloth and carelessness. The men of action and diligence may prefer to meditate in the upright posture—alert, awake, and alive. Men of sloth or of waning strength may have little choice in the matter; and they, perhaps, will wish to meditate lying down.

Heaven is not concerned, and therefore man should be concerned only with results. Good results are achieved while sitting up. The use of a blanket or a piece of silk in the chair of meditation will, of course, act as an insulator against intruding vibrations, if the supplicant is careful to select one of the color rays indicated in my first discourse on meditation. A stick of pleasant incense or floral fragrance may help to clear the atmosphere of undesirable odors. Music may be used or dispensed with, according to the inclination of the meditator.

Prayers or decrees[1] can be used prior to the period of meditation. The ascended masters know that for mankind, caught as they are in the snares of human feelings and thoughts, a decree session given in full voice before the meditation period will serve to insulate, to protect, and to harmonize the four lower bodies so that each lifestream can be best prepared to receive the fruits of his own meditation.

It should be understood that at inner levels, according to the teachings of the Great White Brotherhood, a period of meditation is regarded as a journey into the temple. We call this temple the Temple Most Holy; and it is, in a very real sense, the laboratory of the Spirit.

Man is dual. His Higher Self is created in the divine image and it abides in perfection. The lower self, with its personality complexes, its subconscious forcefield—cause, effect, record, and memory—is a maze of intricate and disturbing arrangements. Yet within this id, or "identity-density," must be anchored the bond upon which God depends for the climactic fulfillment of individual creation and the final raising of the individual into union with his Real Self.

This concept may be a bit difficult for some to understand. I would suggest, rather than reject it because it does not fit a specific dogma, that each chela who cannot fully accept or understand it "put it on a shelf" (as he ought to learn to do about many things he cannot accept at first) until his understanding has improved. Thus his steps on the spiritual path will not become strewn with stones of rejection which he must eventually retrace and pick up, one by one, in order to complete his journey.

Let us make clear that it is the dual nature of man that must be harmonized. Let us outline that labor in the Temple Most Holy is needed in order to prove and to improve the relationship of the individual to the Higher Self. Are men irreligious? Are they lacking in faith? Are they bored with life's experiences? Let them learn to travel the most thrilling pathway of the ascent—the ascent through meditation upon the Christ consciousness above and upon the Divine Presence above.

That which is below must enter the Temple Most Holy. It must come as it is. The outer faculties must first be cleansed and charged with the vibrations of the higher so that you may enter the temple, but the transfiguration of the whole man cannot take place all at once. And so you must come as you are, with all of your errors, mistakes, misconceptions, and negative vibrations. You must come intending to correct these outer conditions, to bring them into harmony with the Divine. You must recognize that each meditation period is intended to enfold you in the character of God, and this brings us to the most important point of all.

In order to avoid the awful sin of unrighteousness which can be the worst hindrance to the disciple on the Path, you must learn (1) to accept the character of the Most High God as your own, and (2) to do so without the overpowering sense of pride that lords it over those who have not thus learned to identify with God. You are among the fortunate few to whom is given the knowledge of the path of meditation and holy prayer. You are able to enter the temple of the Brotherhood where you can serve to surround yourselves with the nature of God; but you must not, you dare not, let a sense of loftiness, of an ivory tower, take hold of your consciousness.

Yours is the mission of the Christ, the lowly

Nazarene carpenter. Yours is the role of the humble child in the crèche. You may be surrounded by adoring ministrants—the angelic hosts, cosmic beings, ascended masters, your own Holy Christ Self, the great God Presence— but your recognition among men may be so little that they may even spit upon you. You must be willing, then, to endure any suffering for Christ's sake, for God's sake, and for man's sake.

Your meditation must be for one sole purpose—in order that the beauty of the Divine may come into manifestation within you, that the Higher Image may surround you, and that you may literally become that image. This is the highest teaching which God can impart to man before opening the portal of reality and Self-awareness. Know, then, that each thought that unduly lifts up the self is your worst enemy and that meditation is best accomplished by clearly understanding its purpose. The purpose of meditation, I repeat, is that God above may manifest in man below—as above, so below.

If it is truly God who manifests below, there will be no room in your being for the sin of self-seeking, the desire for achievement, recognition, or competition with others among men. You will know that the strength of divine unity in the body of God upon earth is the requirement of the hour; and you will know by their fruits that those who claim to be great teachers, great leaders, great souls, gurus, and ministers of righteousness—who foster the sin of separation from mankind, who exalt themselves into positions of fame and fortune—are often in danger of having their works burned by the great transmuting fires of the law.

Make no unnecessary karma in your meditations, but learn the path of humility which will
make you great because you already are. This
is the greatness that you share with every son
of God on earth and in the universe. It is the
greatness of the light itself which belongs to all. It
does not weaken your joint-heirship with the
Christ to share it with the mass of illumined
believers. It can only strengthen it; for each son
of God who attains his perfect reunion with God
and his manifestation of God, fulfilling the
command "Be ye therefore perfect, even as your
Father which is in heaven is perfect," is also
enriching the borders of God's kingdom upon the
planet.[2]

How men individually need this, I say! How
the world needs it, the Brotherhood reiterates!
Meditation, then, can be a delight; but you must
school yourself to understand that the Brotherhood is concerned not only with manifestations
of high states of consciousness, but also with the
consciousness of service. This has been drama-
tized in the ideal of the Bodhisattva.[3]

Not all are called or elected to the same
office. Each year a certain number of individuals ascend from this planet under the auspices
of beloved Serapis Bey of Luxor, Egypt; yet not
all candidates for the ascension are destined
for Luxor this year. Each year a certain number
of individuals attain to the state of nirvana.
Each year a certain number of individuals are
healed of dire conditions. Each year so many
are raised a step in initiation, and each year
so many are given their first initiation into

the spiritual hierarchy.

Preparation for progress is needed at all costs, and the suggestions we are making in this series on prayer and meditation are for the expansion of the soul's awareness of God. The Master Jesus said in his final embodiment, "They that be whole need not a physician." Those of you who already know all of these things and do them need not be reminded.[4]

We remind that you may live the more abundant life. We teach new things from day to day; and we clothe the old mysteries in a more palatable form in the hopes that men who on this planet seek to magnify the good in life and pray that nature and nature's God may be made visible unto all will be willing to make any necessary changes in their lives and to accept any new hint from our octave. Thus it is our prayer that the universal love of God may increasingly release men from error's bane, blight, and pain and lift them to the golden sun again.

True knowledge is power.

Graciously, I AM
Kuthumi Lal Singh

12

The White-Hot Heat
of Meditation

Seekers of
Communion Comfort:

One of the greatest desires of God is to give comfort to mankind. The eternal Spirit ever seeks to provide opportunity for a marvelous expansion of consciousness out of the very life experiences of each individual.

It is well known by students of psychology, philosophy, and religion that human nature tends to vacillate; but the many factors involved in mankind's vacillations are not so well known. History cites endless cases of individuals who have changed their minds at the most crucial hour, when nations and even whole continents might have been saved by the staying power of a handful who knew better but did not do better. It is sad but true that human emotion is easily swayed by the shifting sands of mortal opinion.

The great value of meditation upon the higher realms of the Spirit is that communion with the higher conveys grace to the soul and opens the heart to receive God's love. When the individual cherishes God's grace and his love, he provides the means whereby a divine stability, an inspired constancy, may be effectively established within his soul. There is no substitute, then, for the Divine Mediator, the Divine Comforter, or for those sacred moments when the individual communes with the Higher Self.

Meditation is a form of *satsanga*[1] which conveys great and lingering blessings to the seeker.

We have full compassion for the aspirant, but we know that the Lords of Karma from time to time must assist each one on the spiritual path in balancing the debts to life which he has accumulated. This he must do by the fullest use of life's opportunities—which are indeed heaven-sent—although the process may seem painful at times.

Wise is the man who midst the pangs of adversity will recognize that the hand of God is everywhere, speaking through the humblest of persons or the seemingly unimportant matter which may engage his consciousness. If men and women in their meditations will hold the thought that the Most High is constantly working out the salvation of individual men and women by pointing to the beautiful behind the surface appearance of the ugly, by revealing the perfect form behind the nebulous and formless concept, they will discover the key to lasting happiness through the efficient use of the immaculate concept.

Meditation is a time set apart from the mortal drift, from vacuums of thought and vapid ideas which have made unfortunate impact upon the consciousness. Meditation is a time when life can convey the highest good, the summum bonum of reality, to the communicant. Why do men and women, devotees of the greatest classical music, span with the fingers of their minds and imaginations the ritual of infinite harmonies expressing through the symphonies and fugues of earthly composers and their orchestrations? Is it not because without definition there cannot be conveyed a higher order of harmony to the consciousness?

Meditation ought not to be prescribed by

the meditator. He may choose a subject of the higher order upon which to reflect; but he should always permit the hand of God to lead him in thought, that the meditations of his heart and mind may be directed exclusively by his Holy Christ Self and mighty God Presence, I AM.

Among the dangers in meditation which many have faced is the altogether human penchant for the psychic (because it is so readily available) and the wish to find a unique teacher in the higher realms or perhaps a "spirit guide" who will convey some exclusive concept which one can then parade before his fellowmen.

If the aspirant for higher meditation will only understand that the childlike simplicity and trust of the seeker enables him to contact the reality of the living God, he will cease to be led by the curious elements of his own lower nature into the byways of ego-centered ventures that can never reward him with the spiritual bliss that his soul craves. For even as God's love flows to all in equal measure, he does convey a specific motif of exquisite and unique beauty to each monad according to his infinite purposes.

Each snowflake falling from the sky manifests its own fluffy radiance of cryptographic imprint, of geometric perfection, of unique hope, and of the grace of God's beauty. How much more, then, can the soul that is receptive to the Eternal Fount, to the pressure of the flow of Cosmic Identity, remit its darkness by transmutation into pure light?

No fear should enter the consciousness of the aspirant who would commune with God; for was it not spoken of old, "They shall not hurt nor

destroy in all my holy mountain, saith the
Lord"?[2] The meaning of this phrase is that in man's
rising from the plains of consciousness unto the
summit heights, no evil can befall him nor any
plague come nigh his dwelling as long as the purity and grace of the Spirit of God and of communication with him is maintained.[3] For in the Presence of God, in his holy mountain, man enjoys
total immunity from the world and the full protection of the light. The purpose of meditation,
then, is to keep him centered in that Presence.

Error intrudes through the ego and through
the rebellion of the astral marauders, children of
darkness, "wandering stars to whom is reserved
the mist of darkness forever."[4] Only when men
come to the light can the light give them their freedom, and the forever referred to here is as long as
men remain bound by darkness. The tenure can
vary from a moment to aeons in the case of some
recalcitrant identities. Some men have lost their
souls and become "castaways" through missed
opportunities and the failure to recognize the
perspective of reality for themselves.[5]

We wait with bated breath the magnificent
God-expression of the soul who brings himself to
God in meditation, prepared to accept the en-
thralling but subtle beauty of God-reality which
exists all around him. The consciousness must be
prepared in order to meditate properly; therefore, in this series we are attempting to convey to
the sincere disciple of the heavenly light some
realization of the natural order of things.

Meditation upon God, communion with
God, is not an unnatural state; it is the naturalness of cosmic law which supersedes all lesser

manifestation and remains permanent when all else expresses the quality of inherent change. The immutability of divine law and the fervor of the soul in application to express the perfection of the Deity generate a white-hot heat. This pulsation of the sacred fire waxes stronger and stronger as the soul, taking measure of its past experiences in the realm of form, contemplates for the first time, and then many times thereafter, the meaning of transcendent reality.

What man is, what man has been (what he is expressing and what he has expressed in the past) is not that which man in reality is and what he will become (what he can express and what he will express in the future, namely God). Hope is given new impetus as new possibilities are brought to mind. It is not that the old order was fashioned in utter misery or with changing purpose. It is that the eternal order of universal purpose is best served by the straightforward movement that involves itself in the synthesis of the whole man. To move forward in the realm of divine capacities without making full use of conveyed graces is to deprive the soul of its most wonderful contemplative and meditative opportunities.

Life is expansive. The nature of God is to heal the imperfections of mortal expression—to render them immortal—to change the fashion of the old by the outworking of the Infinite within the finite.

I AM, for your greatest opportunity, your humble mentor in the infinite wisdom,

Kuthumi

13

*Merging with
the Impenetrable Light
of the Atom*

Lovers of Universal Calm:

Be still, O my soul, and know that I AM God![1]

One of the most difficult things for any man to do is to become still. The very excitement of life, the activity in the world of form, like the billows of the sea, threatens to engulf the frail bark of man's identity. When man hotly pursues the Divine, he is not utterly free to storm the bastions of heaven by the fervor of constant and devoted meditation. No indeed; for with each outreach toward God, the lingering voices of the astral realm, the desires of the flesh, the failings and fears, and the old records, like gray ghosts of fallen effort, return to plague the mind and to test the devotion of the chela.

The soul that is enthralled by the love of Christ must guard against invoking his love out of the desire to experience its pleasure rather than for the multi-faceted uses to which that love can be put as Cosmic Christ action in the world of form. In the divine romance, the Beloved must be seen and known as the reality of the self, and love itself must be regarded as the means of transmitting the identity of the Beloved into all-enfolding action in the formless as well as in the form world. This is the purpose of the divine romance, and the imitation of Christ is the highest love to which the chela can aspire.

Too often in meditation the feeling of bliss,

joy, or adoration for God becomes a trap to the
aspirant which catches him up in the glamour of
the divine romance. Unless he first calls forth the
proper protection, this state of divine ecstasy can
leave him wide open to the assault of negative
forces who would like nothing better than to
cause him to plummet from his lofty adventure
into a certain morbid despair. The soul who
beholds the wonder of God as the wonder of his
True Self and finds his pleasure in enthroning the
qualities of God within the chalice of his
character is the truly great divine lover.

When El Morya asked us, beloved Jesus and
me, to discourse on these subjects, we made our
entreaty to Pallas Athena, the Goddess of Truth,
and we urged all of the forces of light to work
within our own consciousness so as to draw the
most vivid images and transmit them to the
students with a view toward greater progress for
all.

Meditation is not intended to be entertain-
ment, albeit we admit it can be; but the chela
must be prepared to engage in the constancy of
right meditation even when feelings of bliss are
not present and when the enclosing forces of
negativity seek to oppress the aspirant to divine
contact.

Let darkness surround! The dawn is coming!
The dawn exists. The dawn is within. Let fear
assault! Love is greater. Love is compassion,
even for the seeker. Love seeks to convey itself
into the nether regions of man's darkness. The
Christ—the Christos—the Greater Light must
burst the bonds of shadowed substance, of
wrong thought and feeling. The golden lotus cup

of the Buddha is raised toward the haven of universal comfort.

God watches the seeker; he answers each call. He places himself within the chalice of the seeker's consciousness. God is available. Through meditation upon him there is a raising-up of the eye of the soul to behold God. The Knower, the Perceiver, becomes the known; for the fingers of the Divine reach out and touch in the darkness the upraised hands of the seeker.

The communion of higher meditation can be a lightninglike experience wherein the fohatic powers of Infinite Love enfold and enslave the lover of the Divine until he can no longer extricate himself from his universal destiny. But he has placed himself in this position; he has held his faith that the purposes of God are benign, that the greatest purpose of God is the conveyance of universal reality to the self, and that this must of necessity involve total surrender. For if man would receive all that is real, he must give up all that is unreal.

Serenity cannot manifest so long as the individual is surrounded by fear or vacillation. Only as man outpictures the attributes of the Divine does the immutable law express through him. The tangibility of God is the tangibility of his manifestation within. What phenomenon can exceed the manifestation of the universal Lord of life and death, as he appears within the seeking son?

No mission is greater than the mission of unity with God. Contemplation and meditation set forth these goals before the mind and heart of the contemplator. He who loves God is beloved of God. The human sea is like a mist of darkness; and the falling arc of descendant reality, the mighty light that shines in the darkness of men, touches the droplets of individuality that rise into the atmosphere. Moment by moment their opacity is reduced, their translucency is transmitted into transparency; and the whole is rendered a miraculous crystalline sphere of reflected light merging with the impenetrable light that is within the heart of every atom—of every sun—of every child whom God hath made.

Prayer is invocative; meditation is convocative. The Word goes forth; and the Word is the burning power of the Spirit that abides in the flesh but consumes it not, that transforms it, that raises the whole man, with his passion for reality, vibrationally, emotionally, mentally, etherically, and spiritually. For the entire being of man must be touched by the power of truth, and truth is the nature of God. The seeker for truth will find it within as he contacts the mind of God in nature, in himself, and in the disciples of all ages who have merged their consciousness into meditation upon the One.

That there is no higher religion than truth must be proven by every man through the science of meditation. You cannot fellowship with darkness and find light. Scientific meditation includes the drawing-apart from worldly fellowship, from old communions of coarseness, and the setting-aside of daily periods when man, facing the dawn of his own Spiritual Self, can watch the rising sun of perfection appearing in the sky of his own consciousness. When it comes to the zenith, it performs its perfect work of flooding the whole sphere of identity with the universal light.

We are made aware again and again of how individuals, in their search for God, ponder weighty intellectual tomes as though conveyance could thus be made of the Universal Mind. The Universal Mind, beloved ones, is just as strong in man when it remains undefined as it is when it takes a relatively definitive expression (for all form expressions of the Deity must be relative to the Whole).

"The Spirit of the Lord is upon me. He has anointed me to preach the gospel to the poor, to bring glad tidings of good things to all people."[2]

Let men understand that the universality of God wipes away the tears of separation that prevent men from seeing their place in the universal scheme. You must meditate in order to bring to God the fruits of your own unique experience. You must convey to him your joys and your sorrows. Because his nature is sublime, he will wipe away all tears from your eyes, all blindness from the heart, and crown you with the radiance of the Christed One, of the victorious Buddha, the unfolding spiritual flower.

Gratefully, I AM

Kuthumi

14

Universal Light
Carries Man to the Altar
of Transmutation

To All Who Seek Him:

The old phrase "If the hill will not come to Mahomet, Mahomet will go to the hill"[1] reveals a law that, when understood, imparts great blessing.

The temptation to feel bored with life, which sometimes seeks to ride in during meditation, is a sinister vibration calculated to destroy the concentration, devotion, and profit of each meditative session with God. If one is to meditate upon God, how can one be bored with such a colossal idea as life, which *is* God? Yet the carnal mind goes on to say that all of this "boredom" could be relieved by travel in search of God.

To this I say emphatically, Is not God everywhere? Yes, the mountain can and does come to man; for the love of God, when contacted in meditation through faith and understanding of his omnipresence, will break through and fire the mind and heart with joys too numerous to mention, vistas too beautiful to describe, and stairways lost in the transcendental mist of cosmic hope.

God will come to you. You have but to call, but your faith must be firm. You must be willing to transmit your cares and considerations to him. You must free yourself from your burdens. You must merge with the light. The light is real, and the Summit of every man brings him to the light.

The light is universal and consummate. It binds up the total expression of the individual and carries him as he is to the altar of transmutation.

Here the fiery love of God consumes the passing trivia of life and suffuses the bud of the unfolding, glowing Divine Person with pulses of light from the heart of his Creator. There is enough of God to go around. You need have no fear that you may draw too much of him, but only that you may draw too little. In him the greatest commodity in all the universe is offered to every man; yet people, submitting to ignorance and allure, look elsewhere for courage, strength, power, wisdom, and friendship. Decrying the hopeless situations they find and the alternate patterns of sunlight and shadow, the ups and downs of daily existence, men turn passionately to God in one moment and in another to the world.

The great Master Jesus said, "No man can serve two masters."[2] Either this Master Presence of Life, your eternal God Presence I AM, is sufficient for the day's evils or you must let the world be your teacher.[3] If God be sufficient, if the everlasting love of the Father be enough, then let men no longer whine, but commune. Let your meditations be acceptable in the eyes of God; for they are designed to reach up unto him, to convey your aspirations and your hopes, and to form the matrices of your desires according to your highest understanding in order that God may fill them with the substance of immortal love.

Do not qualify your aspirations with immortality before they are tried by the fires of

God's love. If they be frail and unworthy of the fire of eternal creation, the fire will burn through the substance and melt with fervent heat the unworthy matrix.[4] Let it go into the furnace of God's love; for a new, glowing, and more beautiful form will come forth to hold a still greater measure of Infinite Love.[5]

Grace conveys, grace upholds, grace magnetizes beauty. All that men do, however, must be to mold them into a vessel for the use of God. If one would pray, "Lord, make me an instrument of thy peace," then he must be prepared to submit to the will of peace. The handiwork of service must be offered generously without thought of reward or personal glamour. As long as the servant or the disciple goes forth with the longing in his soul for worldly recognition, just so long will he delay his real service to God and to man.

Surrender must be beyond recall. Those who hold back part of the treasure and pleasure of life, those who still desire to live exclusively for themselves, fail to understand the law of sweet surrender. Does man surrender to God? Can God do more than surrender in return? Can he fail to recognize that the soul has offered himself in the service of the King? Shall not the King, then, empower him as his representative, as his ambassador? Shall the King not fight all of his battles and, by the Spirit of absolute justice, provide him with all of his rewards?

Meditation, then, is enhanced by surrender under guard. Surrender under guard means a consecrated surrender to the purity of love, to the beauty of love, to the realization of love, to

the joy of love, to the strength of love, and to the
tones of love.

Love is a melodious, harmonious sound. It
is the impulse of God's own consciousness; it
impinges upon the universe and trembles the bars
of eternal creativity. The turning of the universes
creates the music of the spheres. The God-
passion caught up in the Macrocosm evokes its
responses in the microcosm of men's hearts.
They cannot be kept apart from God. They
cannot be kept apart from one another. The
strength of righteousness and justice that exalteth
a nation exalteth the individual. Compassion
does not compromise evil. Compassion upholds
Good, and the pinnacle of example for all is the
divine life.

The justice of God is revealed in the statement of Christ "And as ye would that men should
do to you, do ye also to them likewise."[6] The
interaction of men's deeds must be examined by
the careful ones. Full of concern for each leaf in
creation, these understand the passion of the
Cosmic Mother. These understand the outreach
of the soul into nature and into all things that
contact the immediacy of one's world, together
with all things that are in the far-flung worlds.
Just as the "Great Computer" may be faithful in
many things, so can the one who submits his
consciousness to the will of God be faithful to
surrender to him (to the law of perfection that
God has placed within the beloved Son) the
keeping or "computing" of his tranquil course to
fulfillment and mastery.

You were not born to be a glob of meaning-
less putty. Precious ones, God made you in his

own image in order that you might express that
image in the beauty of the here and now. He did
not intend that you should wait for some far
distant time to receive, through his infinite compassion for you, the highest gifts of himself. As
you meditate upon him and call upon him, you
open the door to all of the Good that the universe
holds in abeyance for you.

The world is in tumult. Men cry out for
social justice. The answer of God through the
great Lords of Karma shows consistently that as
men give, so shall they receive. Those who are
surrounded with fears as to the future would do
well to understand that universal law does not
err, but picks up in the silent meditations of
men's hearts every fear, every doubt and frustrating sense; and the things that men fear may
indeed come upon them.[7]

Let them understand conversely that the
things that they love, the beauty that they wish
to evoke, the servant of Universal Order that
they wish to become, all that belongs to God is
within their outreach. With the fingers of their
hands, they can touch the face of God and feel in
that firm and tender reality the glory that was
once inscribed upon themselves. For the divine
image remains in glowing fire as their own
individualized God Presence, I AM. This sweet
form of infinite reality, connecting them with
every part of life, remains unchallenged as the
Ageless Father guarding the manifestation of
reality for each servant-son.

When you rise in your meditations, let it not
be to astral cities or to psychic episodes! But let
your aspirations soar beyond the stars to the

realm of universal ascended master love right
where God is, for

> Where your treasure is,
>   there shall your heart go; [8]
> Where your desire is,
>   there do your energies flow;
> When you hitch your wagon to a Star,
> You find out who you really are.

Devotedly, I AM

Kuthumi

*"How Much of God
Can You Draw Down
into the Chalice of Self?"*

To All Who Toil Not
in Holy Things, but Love:

As the gentle lilies grow
In swampland here below,
So the fashion of the soul
Sheds its golden glow.[1]

   Meditate, levitate, precipitate!
   All shadows but conceal.

    Your heart communes,
    Your soul now blooms,
    Derived from all that's real.

The fashions of meditation may vary according to the individual's previous training. The effects of outer experience and the manner in which the jumble of human thoughts and feelings is piled into the hopper of the memory determines the relevant profit which the soul may receive from its meditations.

The consecrated use of the violet fire of freedom's love, the proper anointing of the being with the unguent of prayer, and the determined communion by decrees all provide a means whereby meditation can unfold and expand the boundaries of individual reality. Those who seek the summit of themselves come to us with sacks of wisdom and ignorance. The ignorance we remedy with knowledge; the wisdom we examine and correct, adding thereto from the storehouse of heaven's experience.

I wish to stress to every devotee who yearns to find the happiness of divine reality that he must take into account his own past sowings. I do not say that this process should be a burden; on the contrary, through the understanding created by considering one's near and far past, individuals can avoid the pitfall of overconcern for themselves. Then they can return to the heart of cosmic purpose by determinately recognizing the fact that wherever they are, they are, and nothing will help them so quickly as to move forward in the light.

Long ago in Palestine Jesus said, "But many that are first shall be last; and the last shall be first."[2] This means that many whose karmic burden is heavy but whose yearning to do God's will is great will move forward more rapidly than those whose burden may be lighter. "Wherefore I say unto thee, her sins, which are many, are forgiven; for she loved much: but to whom little is forgiven, the same loveth little."[3] The soul that has done much good and is aware of it may complacently join the ranks of the hare, while those who have made many errors, by their very intense longing for correction, sometimes join the ranks of the tortoise and win the race ahead of time.[4]

Let all express equal concern to throw off the packs of troubles that they have long carried upon their backs and to do this daily, taking care that there remains no residual re-creation of old errors and morbid feelings. Let all learn to enter into their daily meditations with a view to extending the benefits of their sessions with God not only to friends and neighbors, to relatives and loved ones, but also to a whole wide waiting world—a pool of hearts to whom in many cases the blessing of perception has not yet been given.

Have you considered the fact that many good-hearted people in the world are bound in ignorance, their energies involved in self-commiseration and the longing for comfort from their fellowmen? Even if they were given all that they think they should have, many of them would not know what to do with it. Therefore, your meditation should include appeals to God for wisdom and the wisdom to interpret the directions that heaven releases in response to your calls.

Your meditations are a two-way communication system to God. The darkness and opacity of tomorrow is relieved by the blazing light of truth that lives today in your consciousness. The past vanishes in a burst of service. Each day as the fires of the sun flash over the eastern horizon, God conveys his kiss of peace to you. A luminous orb of opportunity glowing in the light of today promises no dullness or ache of aging, but only a planned planting of the good seed from the Master Sower's own hand which will bear in good time the fruit of a beautiful tomorrow.

Men in their vain imaginings have often said of the world and the banal things thereof, "They do not exist!" There is a certain spirit of smugness abroad in the land which causes men to justify the position of denying the existence of the material world with all of its pressing problems. Refusing to allow that either God or man has created the very conditions which they deplore, they conclude that these conditions do not exist. Going one step further in their proud logic, these individuals conclude that they are therefore not responsible for the world in which they live, for the karma they have made, or for God's energies which they have misqualified.

The manifold works of imperfection which are the heritage of the race exist through misunderstanding and error. Their days shall be shortened because of the mercy and love of God. These things are passing and they will pass, but we will be changed from glory unto glory because the Spirit of Life has decreed it. Man has imprisoned the lightning of the Immortal Splendor. He alone with God must set it free. But withal, students of the light should be wise to realize that the carnal mind ever seeks a means of escape from responsibility and reality.

We have observed sessions of meditation where among the communicants some peep out of one eye to see what others are doing—where the ego seeks the approval of those seated nearby. Yet in the great schools of the Brotherhood where true meditation is taught, the lesson is always given and the question asked: "How much of God can you draw down into the chalice of self? How much of his love can you send out today to relieve the distress of the world? How much can you give away because you have drawn more than you need?"

"My cup runneth over" was an expression which the Psalmist learned in the inner schools of the Brotherhood.[5] When you deal with the energies of God, you are dealing with the limitless treasury of infinity. You are dealing with

the Brotherhood whose energies are renewed
because all that they have is given in service and
in love. You are dealing with the unlimited
power of cosmic kinetics. God trembles on the
brink of your cup; and his trembling is the
pulsation of greatest hope, greatest faith, greatest
love. He wills it so and it must be done. For you
join him in his meditation; you provide the
avenue for the open door of his consciousness
into the world. You merge your flame with the
God flame that the fire upon the mountain may
flow his molten lava down to the plain below, a
volcano of seething action that will cut through
the astral maya, the glamour, illusion, karma,
and confusion of the world.

Men who have repudiated the Divine
Mother through the slaughter of the innocent
seek to deceive, if possible, the very elect and to
defy the edicts of heaven.[6] These are not worthy
to unloose your shoe latchet.[7] The words of
Christ before Pilate must be remembered: "Thou
couldest have no power at all against me, except
it were given thee from above."[8] Thus there is no
power anywhere save that which is derived from
God. The power of a heart of love is sufficient to
sustain each man until the flame of his reality can
become a coal from the altars of heaven.

The ascended masters' realm is tangible and
real. It is a city above the astral clouds where the
face of God is seen forever. There is no room for
shadow in this universal open-skyed place where
I AM that ye may be also.[9] The germs of
delusion, spewed out into the world and per-
meating the astral, provide a curtain of horror
that separates man from God, that separates

man, through illusion, from reality. It has been said: "From the unreal lead me to the real. From darkness lead me to light. From death lead me to immortality."[10]

Let the meditations of your heart be acceptable in the sight of God.[11] Let the compassion of your meditations refuse to be enmeshed in human sympathy. God is the portion of every man who will receive him. His fire warms the hearth of identity. His beauty, as a soft wind, releases the fragrance of a rose. His grace is as a splendid bird in flight, soaring and dipping with infinite delight. The thoughts of God in form and out of form are thoughts of light. Except ye be born again, ye cannot see the kingdom of God.[12]

O God, open the eyes of men to the new birth, to the realm of the Christed ones! Open the gates of consciousness that they may behold thee! Break the chains of human bondage that they may be free! Lead them by thy light that they may see that every burden is light: It must go free![13] Substance garlanded with hope, with spirituality, wraps its swaddling garment around the world. All that I AM, all that I hope to be, is in thy banner now unfurled, Christ-I-AM-ity.

I shall bless you in your continuing meditation.

Lo, I AM ever in the light,

Kuthumi

16

A Meditation with Kuthumi:
Entering the Temple
of Interior Illumination

Children of Great Faith,

Awake in God this hour,
And come with me
Into the Temple of Interior Illumination.
Apart only from the shell
Of things that seem to be,
Enter then into thy great divine reality.

Long ago when I spake unto
The Brothers of the Holy Order of Saint Francis,
I stirred their hearts to the very depths,
And they walked with me
As in a cloistered consciousness.
This day when so many of you
Are gathered together in one place—
Individuals who have long pursued
The spiritual path
And whose hearts are touched
With the desire for peace—
I say, then, this night
Let the holy drops of the interior peace
Of all those blessed monks
And brothers of holy orders that have ever lived
Descend upon thee.

Many of you, blessed ones,
Have cares of the world thrust upon you
And you are not a part of cloistered seclusion,
But you abide
Full of outer responsibility
And yet trembling

With the longing of the soul
To find entrance into
Those spiritual fortresses of light
Which exist in the reality of your being
And yet have not always opened at your knock
And have not always been contacted
When your heart and cup of being
Was filled with longing.
Let us not engage in speculation
As to the whys and the wherefores of this
But know that this night,
By divine permission,
We are able to hold a specific contact,
By Karmic Board decree,
With your own being
And call you apart
Into a holy and cloistered seclusion
That shall enable you to feel
That mighty sunburst radiance
That is both holy wisdom, holy power,
Holy love, and holy peace.
Drink, then, this cup of peace which I bring.
Drink, then, this Christ peace which I AM.
Drink, then, this opportunity of the hour
And know that the world's density has no power
In thee this hour.
I declare it
And it is done.

The stillness of the angelic hosts
Is building a golden cylinder of light
Around this room.
From the moment that I descended to speak
And stood here upon this spot,
These blessed beings began the process
Of insulating this room and its content

From the vibratory action of mankind's density.
And now we ask
That you also unite with me in thought
And begin a process whereby
You insulate yourselves
In the temple and citadel of your own being
From those thoughts and feelings
Which have hindered your progress
Through the years.

There are some here
Troubled by unwanted thoughts,
Yearning within themselves to escape
From those thoughts,
Desiring to know
A greater measure of Christ peace,
Desiring to feel
A greater sense of compassion.
Let us, then, accept
The amplification of virtue
Which God provides this night.
It is true that the full measure of this
Is in the soul of every man.
But tonight, as I call you apart
And you come with me into the Interior Temple,
You will walk down a cloistered arbor,
And you will see the cells, as it were,
In which sit the spiritual hermits
That exist to the present hour
Agathered there
In separate communion with God
And commingling their love
In higher dimensions—
Forms apart but consciousness is merged,
Consciousness is one.

God in his great unfolding radiance, then,
Knows no dense separation
But enters into the heart of the faithful
To bring to them the sweet essence of the sun,
To bring to them the gentle kiss of the wind,
To bring to them the cleansing purity
Of the water element,
To bring to man, then, the holy fire
That stirs his regenerate nature
As never before.
And so I say
In the name of God's peace,
Let all here forsake
Outer consciousness, outer identity.
Let all here come with me
Into this Temple of Being
With all of its many separate rooms
And behold in the central part of the temple
A mighty altar of light.
Enshrined upon this altar
Is the simple flickering flame of being—
Your being and mine.
Not a separate being but one divine essence.
And as we merge our substance with this flame,
There leaps forth
A ray of golden illumination.
And all can be touched in this Interior Temple
With the radiance of God's golden sunlight
And receive, then,
Especially those who are worthy,
A measured outpouring of holy wisdom's fount.

Brothers of the Golden Robe,
These candidates who plead for admission
Into the Interior Temple of Holy Wisdom

Are indeed they who have pursued the Path
For many a season.
And they have not grown faint
Although they have trembled.
They have sought and they shall receive
The full measure
Of that devotion which they have given.
Precious ones, I give you now
A cup of divine compassion.
Will ye drink it with me this hour?
This compassion is not akin to human sympathy,
It is akin to divine understanding.
It knows the source
Of man's problems and plagues.
It knows the source
Of his density and lack of astuteness.
It knows the source of his troubles
And his troubles that extend
Into his heart, his thought, and his feeling world.
Drinking this compassion,
Give to mankind freedom.
Give to mankind freedom to accept holy truth.
Give them not the pressure, then,
Of your thought
But give them the goodness
Of your love.
Take now, then, this cup which I bear,
The Cup of Peace,
And in this Interior Temple set apart
Drink into God's peace.

God's peace is like a rushing wind.
You are aware
That at the eye of the hurricane
There is a great calm.

Jesus Christ

I am come to send fire on the earth;
and what will I, if it be already
kindled? But I have a baptism to be
baptized with; and how am I straitened
till it be accomplished!

> —Jesus
> *The Gospel According to St. Luke*

Jesus Christ

The "Anointed One" c. 4 B.C.-29 A.D., Nazareth of Galilee,
Palestine; The Saviour, Incarnation of the Word, Avatar of the
Piscean Age, Exemplar of the Redemption through the Individual
Christ Consciousness, Founder of the Community of the Holy
Spirit, World Teacher and Initiator of Souls on the Path of the
Ascension

Lord,
> *Make me an instrument of Thy peace.*
> *Where there is hatred let me sow love;*
> *Where there is injury, pardon;*
> *Where there is doubt, faith;*
> *Where there is despair, hope;*
> *Where there is darkness, light; and*
> *Where there is sadness, joy.*

O Divine Master,
> *Grant that I may not so much*
> *Seek to be consoled as to console;*
> *To be understood as to understand;*
> *To be loved as to love.*
> *For it is in giving that we receive,*
> *It is in pardoning that we are*
> *   pardoned, and*
> *It is in dying that we are born*
> *   to eternal Life.*

> —St. Francis of Assisi

Kuthumi

Koot Hoomi Lal Singh, nineteenth-century Kashmiri Brahman;
the Master K.H., Co-founder of Theosophy 1875, ascended
1889; World Teacher, Master Psychologist, Sponsor of Youth;
incarnated as St. Francis of Assisi 1182-1226, stigmatist, the
'Divine Poverello', Founder of the Franciscans

Kuthumi

*Understand, then, that it is movement
to the great God Self within that is
your salvation in this age, that all
problems of the economy, the ecology,
and the government can be resolved
if you will take only ten minutes each
day to go within and to find your own
God Self, to meditate and to use
the science of the spoken Word
whereby you chant the mantra of the
free: "I AM a being of violet fire—
I AM the purity God desires!" This
is my mantra which I give to you as
your initiation into the Aquarian age.*

—Saint Germain through the
Messenger Elizabeth Clare Prophet

*Decrees are synthesized manifesta-
tions of the heart flame of each one
who decrees. Decrees draw together
and focalize the power of the spoken
Word, the visualization of the Christ
mind, and the rhythm of the divine
pulse.* —Saint Germain, p. 143

Saint Germain

Ascended May 1, 1684, following incarnation as Francis Bacon;
known in the eighteenth century as le Comte de Saint Germain,
'the Wonderman of Europe'; Chohan (Lord) of the Seventh Ray
of Freedom, Hierarch of the Aquarian Age, Sponsor of the United
States of America, Initiator of Souls in the Science and Ritual of
Transmutation through the Violet Flame of the Holy Spirit

Saint Germain

*The key to the understanding of
chelaship is that God is the doer and
that in all works that are wrought
through you, to him be the glory. And
therefore you seek not glory for chela
but only again and again to be reduced
to the diamond point of light, to have
your lesser self and its lesser involve-
ments dissolved, to have the fattened
consciousness thinned, and to have
the self-satisfaction become rather
satisfaction in the home, in the community, in the Path, and in the alignment. Beloved ones, those who
follow me up the mountain know one
thing, that my philosophy is this: Life
is not worth living when it is lived
even for a moment outside of the will
of God.*

—El Morya through the
Messenger Elizabeth Clare Prophet

*I speak of meditations which are
like unto individuals who are afraid
to get wet. They dangle their feet in the
ocean and fearfully, momentarily, and
always prepare to run from the
inundating waves. Meditation, then,
must be entered with a willingness
to go where God goes.*

—Kuthumi, p. 72

El Morya

El Morya Khan, nineteenth-century Indian Rajput prince;
"Mahatma of the Himavat," the Master M., Founder of Theosophy
1875, ascended 1898; Chief of the Darjeeling Council of the Great
White Brotherhood, Guru of the Messengers, Founder of The
Summit Lighthouse; incarnated as Sir Thomas More 1478-1535,
"A Man for All Seasons"

El Morya

Only in selflessness
Can the soul be trusted with
    omnipotence.
When the Lord God knows by the
    proof of action
That the soul can let go and bestow
    upon humanity
Every blessing that it has received from
    on high,
Then he will bequeath to that soul
Limitless energy and the powers
Not only of this world but of many
    worlds.
To learn to give is to learn also
    to receive
And to trust the law
That every thing that thou givest
And every good thing that thou doest
Shall return to thee tenfold
By the wheel of the law of the ten
    perfections.
This is a law which must be trusted
Before it can be tested,
And even in the testing it must be
    trusted.

                    —Gautama Buddha through the
                    Messenger Elizabeth Clare Prophet

            The broad road will narrow, and
            the narrow road that leadeth to eternal
            life will expand as man passes through
            the portals of succeeding tests into the
            trackless dimensions of the Infinite.
                                    —Jesus, p. 36

Gautama Buddha

Prince Siddhartha Gautama of the Kshatriya (warrior) caste,
India, c. 563-483 B.C., Founder of Buddhism, Great Teacher of
Enlightenment through the Ten Perfections, the Four Noble
Truths, the Eightfold Path, the Middle Way; Lord of the World,
the "Compassionate One," Guardian of the Threefold Flame of
Life at Shamballa, Sponsor of Summit University

Gautama Buddha

Allah is the Light
   of the heavens and the earth.
The similitude of His light
   is a niche wherein is a lamp.
The lamp is in a glass.
The glass is as it were a shining star.
(This lamp is) kindled
   from a blessed tree,
an olive neither of the East
   nor of the West,
whose oil would almost glow forth
   (of itself)
though no fire touched it.

Light upon light,
Allah guideth unto His light whom
   He will.
And Allah speaketh to mankind
   in allegories,
for Allah is Knower of all things.
                    —*Al-Qur'ân 'the Koran'*

> *The Word is the burning power of*
> *the Spirit that abides in the flesh but*
> *consumes it not, that transforms it,*
> *that raises the whole man, with his*
> *passion for reality. The seeker for truth*
> *will find it within as he contacts the*
> *mind of God in nature, in himself,*
> *and in the disciples of all ages who*
> *have merged their consciousness into*
> *meditation upon the One.*
>   —Kuthumi, p. 97

Muḥammad

Arabian prophet 570-632, descendent of Abraham through
Ishmael; Messenger of God, the "Slave of Allah," Founder of Islam;
received from Archangel Gabriel the Sacred Book of the *Koran*
'The Reading' of the man who knew not how to read

Archangel Gabriel and Muḥammad

*And there are some among you who
have wondered about your life's calling
and your place in the scheme of things.
I say to you, the design and the matrix,
the direction, has not been forth-
coming simply because you have failed
to forgive. The sin of omission—
not to forgive oneself, not to forgive
another—allows those densities of
the carnal mind to stand between
you and your God, between you and
your realization of the golden rod of
power. So I say, be quick and be
nimble to forgive! and see, then, how
you will also jump over that candle-
stick, that light, that fire of the heart,
how you will be the master of the light,
how you will fulfill your divine plan
and take your leave of this planet in
the ritual of the ascension. And then
if you like you can join me in the
initiations of the Bodhisattvas...*
>   —Kuan Yin through the
>   Messenger Elizabeth Clare Prophet

> *Meditation, then, can be a delight;
> but you must school yourself to
> understand that the Brotherhood is
> concerned not only with manifesta-
> tions of high states of consciousness,
> but also with the consciousness of
> service. This has been dramatized in
> the ideal of the Bodhisattva.*
>> —Kuthumi, p. 84

Kuan Yin

Kuan Shih Yin Tzu Tsai, an incarnation of Avalokiteśvara,
emanation of Amitâbha Buddha; World Mother of Mercy,
Representative of the Seventh Ray on the Karmic Board, Sponsor
of the Evolutions of "The Celestial Empire" of China and the Far
East, Guardian of Mercy's Flame in her Temple of Mercy over
Peking; intercession invoked by the mantra *Oṃ ma ṇi pad me hûṃ*

Kuan Yin

The true devotees are not soiled in mind. Their pure minds dwell on the Lord alone. Through the Guru, they realize the word. And they immerse themselves in the Lord's nectar name. The wisdom of the Guru burns bright in them. And the darkness of their ignorance is dispelled.

Through the medium of the Word the soul doth cross the endless ocean of matter. Lowly Nanak, therefore glorifies His Naam (the Word).

—Guru Nanak
Thus Spake Guru Nanak

Now as the dawn of holy prayer, bridging the chasm between one point and another, radiates its precious light into the consciousness of men, it speaks of the mission that seems to be impossible to those who are wedded to mortal things.

—Jesus, p. 24

Guru Nanak

Hindu prophet of India 1469-1538, called the "Apostle of Peace"; Founder of the Sikhs; set about the reconciliation of Hinduism and Islam in an inspired teaching of one God—*Sat Nam* 'True Name'

Guru Nanak

Lanello

Guru Ma

*Christ has ever abided in me. He has
preached through my consciousness
to all my rowdy and hypocritical
thoughts. With the magic wand of
meditative intuition He has stilled the
storms in the sea of my life and of many
other lives. I was mentally blind, my
will was lame; but I was healed by the
awakened Christ in me. . . . O living
Christ, present in the body of Jesus and
in all of us, manifest Thyself in the
essence of Thy glory, in the strength of
Thy light, in the power of Thy perfect
wisdom.*
　　　　　　　　　　　　　　—Yogananda
　　　　　　　　　　Metaphysical Meditations

*Blessed ones, it is unnecessary for you
to strain or to struggle in order to
achieve communion with God. He
is not far from you; and as near as
heartbeat or thought, he can flood you
with a surge of his renewing strength.*
　　　　　　　　　　　　　　—Jesus, p. 8

Yogananda

Premavatar 'Incarnation of Love' 1893-1952; enjoined by Sri
Yukteswar and Mahavatar Babaji to found Self-Realization
Fellowship, bringing the science of *Kriya Yoga* from the
Himalayan masters to the West; revealed the harmony of science
and religion and the basic oneness of the original Christianity
taught by Jesus Christ and the original Yoga taught by Bhagavan
Krishna

Yogananda

*Let the people understand we are
brethren because we are of the same
Mother.*

*Out of the womb of the Cosmic
Virgin, out of time and space, you
came forth as mighty conquerors, as
teams of conquerors of old—as the
blue race and the violet race. So you
came and so you are one in the light
of Alpha and Omega, the beginning
and the ending, the first and the last—
the one unity. So out of One, many.
So, many is the coming of the One.*

*People of Afra, you must choose this
day whom you will serve! You must
choose to be or not to be. I ask you in
the name of God, will you make your
choice?*
                        —Afra through the Messenger
                        Elizabeth Clare Prophet

*It should be understood that at inner
levels, according to the teachings
of the Great White Brotherhood, a
period of meditation is regarded as
a journey into the temple. We call this
temple the Temple Most Holy; and
it is, in a very real sense, the laboratory
of the Spirit.*
                        —Kuthumi, p. 81

Afra

Patron of Africa, introduced by the Ascended Master Kuthumi
through the Messenger Mark L. Prophet on July 21, 1972, in Accra,
Ghana; the "unknown brother" who offered name and fame to
sponsor the African people; hence known simply as Afra—
a frater, from the Latin, hence "brother" of light

Afra

*I AM not only your Mother but your
very personal friend. I ask you to
take my hand, to take me to your
home, to accept me as your friend—
not as a remote deity, an icon or an
object of irreverence, but simply as the
handmaid of the Lord. Whose Lord?
Your Lord. I AM the servant of the
Lord who lives within you. I AM one
with whom you can be comfortable.
I will sit at your kitchen table and have
a cup of tea with you. I will receive
whatever offering of food that you
prepare; for all is sanctified by love.
I will receive whatever is precious
to you and take it to my heart and give
it back to you with the full consecration of my love.*

> —Mother Mary through the
> Messenger Elizabeth Clare Prophet

*One of the greatest desires of God
is to give comfort to mankind. The
eternal Spirit ever seeks to provide
opportunity for a marvelous expansion
of consciousness out of the very life
experiences of each individual.*

> —Jesus, p. 88

Mother Mary

'Twin Flame' of Archangel Raphael; incarnated in Palestine during
the first century A.D. as the Mother of Jesus Christ; Teacher of
the Science of the Sacred Heart and the Immaculate Conception
of the Christ within Each Child of God; Initiator of the Disciplines
of the Mother Flame; with Raphael, Intercessor of the Healing
Science and the Disciplines of Wholeness in the Temple of Being;
Archetype of New-Age Woman, Sponsor of Incoming Souls

Mother Mary

*I, Michael, promise you that if you
have but a grain of faith that I will
come to you, then, upon that faith.
I will arc my light and show you the
proof of the living Christ—both within
you and within Jesus—and of the
mission that he has given to me to
rescue your soul in this age. O beloved
of God, beloved of God, how I have
known you from the beginning! How
I have been one with you! How I have
come to walk by your side! And in
answer to the prayers of many on
earth, I have been able to keep you
in the way of God.*

—Archangel Michael through the
Messenger Elizabeth Clare Prophet

*Too often in meditation the feeling
of bliss, joy, or adoration for God
becomes a trap to the aspirant which
catches him up in the glamour of the
divine romance. Unless he first calls
forth the proper protection, this
state of divine ecstasy can leave him
wide open to the assault of negative
forces who would like nothing better
than to cause him to plummet from
his lofty adventure into a certain
morbid despair.* —Kuthumi, pp. 94-95

Archangel Michael

Prince of the Archangels, Defender of the Faith, Protector of
the Guru-Chela Relationship, "captain of the host of the Lord"
who appeared to Joshua (Josh. 5:5), "the great prince" prophesied
by Daniel (Dan. 12:1); Protagonist of the Woman and Her Seed
(Rev. 12:7); maintains etheric retreat in the Canadian Rockies
over Lake Louise at Banff

Archangel Michael

If you will precipitate just one particular quality, it will serve as the answer to all of your needs. Now that quality which I am asking you to precipitate is the quality of perfection itself. Do you see, beloved hearts, if you precipitate mere substance and form and then etherialize that substance and form, you are constantly required to measure up to a certain standard. But if you shall precipitate perfection, you have become that standard. Do the scriptures not record how God shall supply all your needs according to his riches in glory by the Christ within you? I say to you of the light—you, beloved hearts! The power of perfection itself will produce, and sustain that which it produces.

—Confucius through the
Messenger Mark L. Prophet

The power of example is the strongest bond in the world that speaks of the Most High having descended to mankind.
—Kuthumi, p. 76

Confucius

K'ung-Fu-tzu, Chinese sage c. 551-479 B.C.; Founder of Confucianism; preserved ancient oriental culture in the *Wu Ching*, the Five Classics; the 'open door' to the ascension of the Chinese people; Hierarch of the Royal Teton Retreat, Jackson Hole, Wyoming

Confucius

*In reality there is no creation,
preservation, or destruction. All is
but the moving stream—the moving
stream of cosmic consciousness. And
the happenings of the moving stream
are in the eye of the beholder. The
onlookers to the River of Life think
that their report is actual when, in fact,
it is not. The only one who knows that
which transpires in the moving stream
is the one who has entered the moving
stream and become the stream. This is
the path of the Buddha. This is the
path where I would lead you, pulling
you gently by the thread—the blue-
white thread of contact. When I pull,
will you come?*

— Padma Sambhava through the
Messenger Elizabeth Clare Prophet

*The nature of the Father is within the
Son. It is within ye all, now and
always. When you reach up hands of
seeking faith and allow the unbroken
prayer of steadfast purpose to act, you
are opening the door to that perfect
understanding that transcends all
mortal sense of limitation.*

— Jesus, p. 43

Padma Sambhava

Eighth-century lama of Tibetan Buddhism known as The Great
Guru; the "Lotus-Born," an emanation of Amitâbha Buddha;
Guru rinpoche 'the precious guru'; the 'open door' of Guru through
the Messenger Elizabeth Clare Prophet

Padma Sambhava

If thou wouldst be the Buddha, thou must know the suffering of life. And therefore the movement of love to be the Saviour, the Saviouress, is based on vision, awareness, enlightenment, the seeing, the knowing. Jesus Christ took his disciples in the Upper Room to this vision of the suffering humanity, and thus each one took the vow of the Bodhisattva to incarnate over and again until this hour of the consummation when those souls could be freed by the dispensation of the ten thousand Buddhas that has come. Beloved ones, some of you have been among those who have taken the Bodhisattva vow.

—Jetsun-Milarepa through the
Messenger Elizabeth Clare Prophet

Once the love of God is rightly understood by any man in any state whatsoever and he responds as prodigal son desiring to see and behold reality, reality cannot be denied unto him. God will come, and he will move in the mysterious ways of a spiritual being and a master of life to raise the individual soul into the ascended state.

—Jesus, p. 28

Milarepa

Tibet's Great Yogi 1052-1135, balanced karma of black magic in nine Meritorious Acts under Guru Marpa 'the translator'; composed 100,000 songs of "The Quintessential Teaching of Practical Buddhism"

Milarepa

Amitâbha Buddha

When you draw, then,
Close to this mighty inrush of cosmic peace,
You will know
When you have the feeling of release
From all tension and dissatisfaction
Of the outer consciousness
That you have reached
The eye of the hurricane
Of God's wondrous peace.
In the stillness and the calmness
Of his heart and mind,
You will possess your souls
And expand the light that is in them
Until the world will not remember you
As you were
But will know you
As you are—
A being of wondrous light and love.

And so, then, tonight
In this Interior Temple of Being—
Your own being—
We will ask that there occur an action
Whereby the sunburst of cosmic victory
Is released there to your vision.
As the sacred Eucharist
Or host upon the altar of the Church,
So the sunburst of the being of God
In all his holy wisdom
Is revealed in Christ loveliness
To the eyes of the beholder.
This stainless holy wisdom
Is the golden rule of the Temple Beautiful,
The Interior Temple of your being.
There is here, then,

Only the snow-white dove
Descending in its great unfolding radiance
And bringing to your consciousness
The feeling of the Holy Spirit.
This is in the Interior Temple of your being.

The Brothers of the Golden Robe
Are with us now.
And as they gather close around,
Raising the canopy of their cape
In such a manner
As to enfold and cover their heads,
You will see
That they are drawing holy wisdom
Around themselves
And gathering the folds of their robe
With their hands
Clutching, then, the fabric thereof
And holding it before their heart.
Their identities, their individualities,
Seem lost to view
And they are as golden flames
Standing round about you—
Holy brothers whose identity is merged
In the great God flame of all life.

This is as it should be.
Mankind's souls are like shining dewdrops
Selected from the sea of life
And lifted up glistening in the sunlight,
Kissed by the wind,
Purified by the glory of heaven reflected
Upon this wondrous globe of watered substance.
The emotional body of man
Must feel a release of all tensions.
And, therefore, I say to you,

In the name of holy wisdom this night,
Take all tensions, all dissatisfactions
With yourself and with others,
All feelings of discomfort,
All feelings of grief,
Of past problems, difficulties, and troubles
And cast them forth from your being,
Cast them forth upon the stones—
The cobblestones that are before you
As you walk in this Interior Temple—
And know that you will be permitted to do this.
For there are they who have volunteered
To take up the burdens you cast forth
And to cast them into the sacred fire.
And if you can lay these burdens down
And not stoop to pick them up again
You can have a permanent healing this night
Of these conditions
So unwanted by your person.
But this cannot be
Unless you receive it in faith,
Unless you stand in full faith
In this Interior Temple of Being.
This cannot be
Unless you accept
The knowing of the Father's love
Into your own heart,
Unless in the full acceptance
Of this measure of heaven's holy wisdom
You recognize that this was a God design
In this Golden Age Conference
Whereby the individuals who gave their energy
Faithfully to the ascended masters
Could receive the blessing of a specific release
Which will enable them

To go forth unto mankind
And assist in the great harvest of souls
Which is coming forth now
As the fields in their whiteness
Express man's need.
And God in his great generosity
Responds to mankind
And declares that it is I who will make peace
Between the divided hearts of men.

For it is in entering in soul consciousness
And immortal essence
Into this Interior Temple of Being
That I will enfold you
In the mantle of my radiance,
The holy wisdom,
The mighty compassion of the ages
That gives to every individual who will
Such holy wisdom that he can become
A light in the world,
A city that is set upon a hill that cannot be hid.
And though men direct arrows at you
Because of the distinguished virtue
Emanating from you,
It will be as naught.
For the shield of faith
Which God will place around you
Shall enable you to walk
Over the consciousness of mankind
In a specific state of elevation.
Elevation of soul must come
In this Interior Temple,
For you are not assembled here
For a mere outer worship
Or a form thing,
But you have entered into the soul of the wind,

You have entered into the soul of the sun,
You have entered into the soul
Of all of the flowers of the world—
Known and unknown.
You have absorbed the holy essence
Of the immortelles known unto Saint Germain
As those unfading floral essences
Created immortally by angelic hands.
You will absorb
In this Interior Temple of your being
The necessary requisites for this hour
To make a God-shining hour
When you go forth to a victory
Which you have hitherto not accomplished.
And this victory which I speak of now
Is an invisible action,
A greater action than that which is manifest.
For that which men see is but a portion
Of that which you shall externalize.
For as you spin
With this holy flame of wisdom
The immortal garments of the eternal essence,
You will find
That revelations are unfolding
Before your consciousness
And the screen of your mind
Which you dare not communicate to mankind—
Not to a single one—
Or breathe a word of it to any living soul.
And you will recall the words of Saint Paul
When he spoke and said,
I knew a man in Christ fourteen years ago
Who was caught up unto the third heaven
And heard unspeakable words
Which it is not lawful for a man to utter.

In the spirit of infinite compassion
And the charge of holy wisdom
Which I am releasing to you this night,
There is a specific action
Of every Brother of the Golden Robe
Upon this planetary body.
Many of these were with me in Assisi
When I ministered unto the people
And builded there a sanctum before men.
But the sanctum sanctorum
Which I builded in my heart
Was a habitation of the vast Spirit
Of the Universal Architect.
It was the selfsame design
That abides in thee.
It is not alone in me
Nor would I be content to be
The only one who could give away
All that God had given me of mortal substance
And receive in return all the immortal substance
Of his blessed being.
I deem myself, then, not a poverello
But I deem myself the richest of all mankind
And I did so then.
For I recognized
That in the Interior Temple of man's being
Is the riches of the Spirit
Which cannot fade away,
Nor be lost,
Nor be destroyed,
Nor be altered,
Nor be changed.
I tell you, blessed ones,
There are many examples before mankind
Of human forgery

But no one can forge their way
By a certificate of inaccuracy
Into the eternal kingdom.
For all that which mankind do
With the pen of their existence,
Writing upon the scroll of immortal being,
Is there until it is made clear
In the holy light of karmic virtue
Whereby every act
Returning to mankind for redemption
Comes again to him
As a "jot and tittle" of the law
Which cannot be removed, then, from his being
Except he offer it unto God
By externalizing a requisite cosmic virtue
To replace that which has been
So subtly ignorant and so subtly evil.

O mankind of earth,
The Interior Temple of thy existence
Is builded around thee
Not in thy fleshly form alone,
But is engraved in thy mighty being—
A tabernacle that reaches above the stars
And places beneath thy feet
The waning moon
Of mankind's emotional struggles,
Giving him the crown
Of the Son, Prince Michael,
Upon his head,
The virtues of God-control whereby he,
Seated, then, in full God-control
In the chariot of being,
Holds the reins thereof in perfect God-design,
Observing every obstruction in his pathway

Before he runs over it
Headlong and hitherto
And seeing the clear way,
The road that leads
Through the sacred-fire essence
To his own freedom.

Mankind, you have an opportunity.
It is not taken from thee.
The great Goddess of Opportunity
With all of her holy wisdom
Stands this night in the atmosphere
Above this room,
Extending, then, specific karmic virtue
To those of you who will accept it
Whereby new opportunities
Shall unfurl before you
In the days to come
That you did not dream existed.
For we still have the power of God
To extend a gratuity to mankind.
And although ascended beings
Are scarce recognized in a relative sense
By the many
That occupy the platform of this earth,
Those of you
Who know our compassionate love
Will understand
That it is our desire to extend to you
Every possible bounty
Which the great cosmic law will permit,
So that as students of the light
Your days ahead
Upon this planetary body
May be days in which you may shed,

More and more,
All elements of human discord
And build around yourself now,
In this seemingly late hour,
All the purity for which your soul longs.
Such is the compassion of heaven.

And now as I muse
Upon the wonders
Of the Interior Temple of Being,
I recall some of the struggles
Of individuals that I have known.
I also recall a cobbler
Who dwelt long ago in Europe
Who was mocked and scoffed at
By the mankind of his city
Because he insisted
Upon perusing the sacred scriptures.
The children of that city
Used to gather and throw stones at him,
Even as he sat in holy prayer.
And the strange thing was
In this specific case
The parents did not seem to care
Or restrain the action of their children.
For it came to pass
That the parents felt,
As did the children,
That his countenance was very ugly.
And it was so from an outer standpoint,
For he lacked physical beauty
And the beauty of a kindly face
But his heart was full of love toward God.
And it is an interesting thing
That this man was later embodied

And entered into the holy orders of the Church
And became a patriarch
And prince of the Church.
And it came to pass
That every one of these young men in this town
Who had thrown the rocks and stones at him
All became priests of the cloth,
And they all were placed under him
In his diocese.
And it came to pass
That many of these came to him
To petition him for spiritual assistance,
And he gave it lovingly
With a pure heart.
And so it came to pass
That in due course of time
These individuals—
Now in a new embodiment
And grown men—
Came to love him
And they returned at a later time
All of the love
Which he had poured out upon them
In a time when they had not recognized his love
And had but cast stones upon him.

So, then, I say to every one of you,
Although at times
You permit yourselves to feel
A feeble connection with your Presence
But you recognize
That this is not the holy law,
This is not the holy intent,
This is not an act of righteousness,
I ask you, then, tonight

To take your hands
And to gather them close to your heart
And to feel in your heart
And around your emotional being
The pressure
Of every wrong thought that is there,
That has ever been there
And yet remains to be transmuted.
Close your hands around about those tightly
And draw them forth from you as far as you can
And then release all of this substance
Into the hands of the violet-flame angels
Who await in the Interior Temple of Being
To take this burden from your life.
Give it to them
Lovingly and gladly.
You will not miss parting with it, I am sure.
And know
That if you will not take it up again
That it shall not trouble you.
For God in his great love
Shall steer you around
Many of the tormenting situations
That otherwise could be deceptive
And cause you great distress.

But there is a holy purpose
In this offering tonight from my heart,
And that purpose is
That as compassion descends
In torrents upon you,
And when the veil is parted
And you begin to see
In this Interior Temple of your being
The very holy strands of God's radiance

Shining forth from you
And you begin to know
That other world of which we are a part—
That precious world
Where the temple of man's true being
Is revealed—
And you feel the sacred-fire core
In all its pulsating essence
And you contact the heavenly beings
In a more than ordinary manner,
Be not aloof to the world to the extent
Of not shewing compassion to them.
Give them understanding, not exaltation.
Do not exalt your ego
Or seek to bring them to grovel at your feet
But let your love be poured out upon them
As in holy orders,
Recognizing not the differences of men
But the similitude of God
In the hearts of men.
So shall the tenets of my holy order
Also come alive again in this day and age.
And the Christ shall be glorified,
And the Christ shall be magnified,
And the Christ in you shall expand,
And the holy threefold flame shall expand
And holy wisdom will come again
To the screen of life.
It will come to the fore in you.
And so God in his mighty compassion
Will make thee
An instrument of his peace.
And so God in his holy compassion
Will make thee

An active participant in his kingdom—
A holy thing born of cosmic flame.

In this Interior Temple of Being,
If you have discovered that
Which I long for you to discover,
You will long muse
Upon the realities
That you have discovered
And you will long muse
Upon the unrealities
Which you had previously thought were so real.
Let these dragons, then,
Be cast out of your consciousness
Back into the lair of nothingness
And let the Christ image
Be enthroned, exalted, lifted up.
May the Spirit of the Great White Brotherhood
Surge through thee
Now and always
In a release of holy illumination's flame.
And may this Golden Age Conference
Go down in cosmic history
As the beginning in many hearts
Of a new sense of righteousness
Stemming from the old sense of the creative image
That in the beginning shone forth
The holy goodness of God.
You cannot change that, if you will.
You can dwell in the house of flesh
And transgress God's laws
But you can never change the pristine image
Which he himself holds
Immaculately for all.

I bless you and seal you
In the name of the Cosmic Christ
In the Interior Temple of your being.
May you dwell there
In the House of God
Forever.

Kuthumi

Saturday, July 25, 1964
Saint Germain's Golden Age Conference
Los Angeles, California

III

The Way
of the Science
of the Spoken Word

*by Saint Germain
and El Morya*

17

*The Power
of the Spoken Word*

Gracious Friends of Freedom,

When we contemplate methods of God realization, we dare not exclude the power of the spoken Word.

For many years the so-called orthodox religions have used ritual and form, together with spoken mantras.[1] In the West these have been called responsive readings, for they require the response of the congregation, or audience participation. In some instances the prayers of mankind have become vainly repetitious and devoid of meaning; but I for one would rather see individuals involved in rote than enmeshed in the wrong kinds of vocalized expression.

It is fitting that men should comprehend the proper use of decrees. Jesus once said: "Every idle word that men shall speak, they shall give account thereof in the day of judgment. For by thy words thou shalt be justified, and by thy words thou shalt be condemned."[2] Decrees are not careless words; they are careful words. And the patterns which we recommend are invocative of the highest good for man.

Decrees are generally composed of three parts, and they should be thought of as letters to God:

(1) The salutation of the decree is invocative. It is addressed to the individualized God Presence of every son and daughter of God and to those servants of God who comprise the

spiritual hierarchy. This salutation (the preamble to the decree), when reverently given, is a call that compels the answer from the ascended ones. We could no more refuse to answer this summons in our octave than could your firemen refuse to answer a call for help in yours. The purpose of the salutation, then, is to engage immediately the energies of the ascended masters in answering the body of your letter to God which you so lovingly vocalize individually or in unison.

(2) The body of your letter is composed of statements phrasing your desires, the qualifications you would invoke for self or others, and the supplications that would be involved even in ordinary prayer. Having released the power of the spoken Word through your outer consciousness, your subconscious mind, and your superconscious, or Higher Self, you can rest assured that the supreme consciousness of the ascended masters whom you have invoked is also concerned with the manifestation of that which you have called forth.

(3) Now you come to the close of your decree, the acceptance, the sealing of the letter in the heart of God, released with a sense of commitment into the realm of the Spirit whence manifestation must return to the world of material form according to the unerring laws of alchemy (the all-chemistry of God) and precipitation.[3]

Those who understand the power of the square in mathematics will realize that when groups of individuals are engaged in invoking the energies of God, they are not merely adding power by the number of people in the group on a one-plus-one basis, but they are entering into a very old covenant of the square which squares the release of power to accomplish the spoken Word by the number of individuals who are decreeing and by the number of times that each decree is given.

We heartily recommend individual decrees to accomplish untold blessings in the lives of those who will discipline themselves in this ritual of invoking light to a darkened world. But group decreeing, when accompanied by an intense visualization of the good desired, is more efficacious on a world scale than individual decreeing and will result in a speedy response to those engaged in it, not only to themselves but also on behalf of all mankind.

It should be borne in mind that whenever Good (God) is invoked in the world of form, surrounded as the world is today by a great accumulation of mortal effluvia, the Good (the light) that is released from on high in answer to the call (because of the high frequency of the vibrations of the light) is automatically opposed by the negative vibrations already existing in the atmosphere of the earth (because of the low frequency of these vibrations).

Rhythm is also important in decrees. Proper rhythm creates a most penetrating projection of spiritual vibrations that will magnetize all over the planet the qualities of God that are being invoked through the decrees. The momentum of these waves that form undulating circles over the planetary body creates an intensification of light wherever devotees come together to participate in a like endeavor.

The laws governing the manifestation and distribution of physical light also apply to the flow of the currents of spiritual light. Spiritual qualities are distributed around the planetary body from every radiating focus of ascended master love. Let no one feel, then, a sense of separation in his service to hierarchy; for by the power of decrees issued forth at any point upon the earth's surface, the currents of light, life, and love from the heart of God can be unleashed as electrical, radiating waves to make their impact in the world and bring back to the invoker the God-ordained response.

The statement "Thou shalt decree a thing and it shall be established unto thee"[4] is an ancient maxim that sets forth the law governing decrees. For man, created in the image of God, has the selfsame power to actuate which was used by God "in the beginning" when he said, "Let there be light!" and there was light.[5] We know full well that individuals who come into our meetings and encounter these decrees for the first time without understanding the laws governing them or the beautiful results that can be obtained through their use can well come under the influence of certain negative forces and entities in the world that quite naturally are diametrically opposed to the use of dynamic decrees.

Too frequently individuals who stress their desire for quiet meditation fail to take into account that there is a time and a place for quiet meditation, a time and a place for prayer, and a time and a place for decrees. All three can be used in religious service. All three can be used in the home, individually, or in groups, as one desires. But one form of worship is not a substitute for the other.

We release this information in this *Pearl of Wisdom* because of the world need for the ascended masters' teachings on the subject. After all, consciousness is one. The individual who dwells in God can pour out his heart to God in prayer, in song, in decrees, or sit silently meditating upon an aspect of Deity. Thought precedes worded expression, or at least it should. Therefore, to meditate or to think upon God is one way of expressing him. Decreeing is another.

When the children of Israel brought down the walls of Jericho, it was by a great shout,[6] a great use of the consummate power of divine energy. The sinister force has perverted this knowledge, which has been a part of the forte of the teachings of the Great White Brotherhood for thousands of years. The black power movement and some Communist groups have taken to training young people in the wrong use of this law involving the power of the spoken Word. Their followers chant in unison and in rhythm, thereby summoning or magnetizing power and projecting it forth upon a vibratory wavelength that is charged with personal and group hatred. The effect of these momentums of mass misqualification can be disastrous upon those who encounter them; for when correctly used, this power did bring down the walls of Jericho.

Because decrees are of such great benefit to mankind, we urge that those who in the past may have failed to appreciate fully the significance of decrees, those who may have taken a position against them, shall reconsider their stand in the light of the cosmic knowledge which I have herein released. Also, we recommend that the members of our sanctuaries and all who are connected with us through the *Pearls of Wisdom* shall make a very real effort to understand the facts concerning the subject of decrees.

Decrees are synthesized manifestations of the heart flame of each one who decrees. Decrees draw together and focalize the power of the spoken Word, the visualization of the Christ mind, and the rhythm of the divine pulse. When you decree, you are releasing into space divinely qualified energy charged by your invocation with the power of the ascended masters which goes forth to do its perfect work for the amplification of the power of light upon the entire planet.

I can say little more than that which was spoken of old: "Prove me now herewith, saith the Lord of hosts, if I will not open you the windows of heaven and pour you out a blessing, that there shall not be room enough to receive it."[7]

The proper use of decrees takes practice. Individuals should not expect that the first time they make a call, the very perfection of the universe will sweep away all of the accumulated debris of their lives. Proper decreeing is an art; and as one gains greater proficiency, he will find it possible to speed up his decrees—that is, he will be able to speed up the rate at which they are given. He will also be able to understand what is taking place as he speeds them up; for this acceleration, by raising the rate of his own electronic pattern, throws off and transmutes negative thoughts and feelings in his world.

Oh, what delight and peace you can bring to your family, to your friends, and to yourself through the proper use of decrees! What a boon to freedom! How gloriously the world can be changed for the better! After all, blessed ones, Nature herself is not always silent. God speaks in thunder, in lightning, and in the wind;[8] and the chattering of the many birds through the world, like the crickets in the swamp, certainly raises the decibels.

By the power of the Word the earth was framed,[9] and by the power of the Word the freedom of man shall be dominantly asserted in God's name. Use your decrees! Fear not the opinions of men, for the hierarchy has spoken and those who heed will profit.

For your valiant freedom in the light, I AM

Saint Germain

*The Dispensation
of the Violet Flame*

Chelas Who Would Also Come to Darjeeling:

Mankind living in the world today assume that recorded history is what it is and that it cannot be changed. They have not reckoned with the violet transmuting flame.

This flame is the energy of the sacred fire that is the gift of the Ascended Master Saint Germain to chelas of the will of God in this age. The dispensation for the release of the violet flame into the hands and use of the students in this century came forth from the Lords of Karma because Saint Germain went before that august body to plead the cause of freedom for and on behalf of mankind. He offered to the Lords of Karma the momentum of the violet flame garnered within his heart chakra and within his causal body as a momentum of light energy to be given to mankind that they might experiment with the alchemy of self-transformation through the sacred fire.

The violet flame has always been used in the retreats of the Great White Brotherhood situated on the etheric plane—the highest plane of Matter—where the ascended masters preside, receiving only the most worthy chelas for instruction and training in the way of initiation. Those who were found worthy—adherents of the various religions, members of secret societies, communicants of the flame in the mystery schools—were given the knowledge of the violet flame after having proved themselves to be selfless as both receivers and givers of freedom on the path of soul liberation.

Thus the violet flame was reserved for the privileged few up until the time when Saint Germain came before the Lords of Karma with the proposal to make the knowledge and use of the violet flame available to all mankind. He boldly stated before the Court of the Sacred Fire, arguing as the advocate for earth's evolutions, that the violet flame would revolutionize the human race and make of that race a divine race of God-free beings.

Indeed, Saint Germain envisioned an "I AM race"[1] being raised up as the forerunners of the seventh root race under the Great Divine Director. This blessed master of freedom who had sponsored the birth of the nation called the United States of America—this guardian of the Christ consciousness who had walked the earth as the protector of Mary and Jesus, this Saint Joseph, this Uncle Sam[2]—foresaw the land of America from north to south, and eventually the entire hemisphere, as the land that was destined to be a haven for the Divine Mother and her progeny.

Inasmuch as he was destined to be the Master of the Aquarian age and the God of Freedom to the earth, the Lords of Karma agreed to the master plan with the following stipulation. First they would release the violet flame to a certain nucleus of devotees in embodiment who would vow at inner levels to use that flame honorably for the blessing and the freedom of all life. If this experiment proved successful, they would allow the knowledge of the flame to be made available to the masses.

I am here to tell you that the dispensation could never have been granted for chelas to invoke this flame outside the retreats of the Great White Brotherhood had it not been for the fact that Saint Germain offered upon the altar of humanity the collateral of his own personal momentum of the energies of freedom garnered within his soul for thousands of years. For you see, when the Lords of Karma granted the dispensation through the intercession of this anointed one, they were fully aware that, given free will and given mankind's propensity to misuse that free will, it was altogether possible that certain numbers among mankind would misuse these sacred energies as they had done in the past in the days of ancient Lemuria and Atlantis. Were this to occur, someone would have to make up the difference.

Saint Germain understood this principle of cosmic law only too well. For the sake of the few and eventually the many who would make resplendent use of the violet flame, he was willing to forego and to sacrifice that portion of his momentum that would be misused and to chalk up that misuse as a necessary expenditure in the laboratory of mankind's consciousness. He was thereby in effect underwriting the experiments not only of the alchemists of the sacred fire with whom he had personally worked through the centuries, but also of the populace who would both use and misuse the alchemical fires ere coming into the enlightenment of the Christ mind and that centeredness in the Christ flame which is necessary for the responsible use of the violet flame.

Now you who are living in the advancing decades of the century are the beneficiaries of this legacy of Saint Germain bought with a price[3]—the overwhelming love of the Master Saint Germain, whose love for you even before you took embodiment was such that he was willing to lay down a portion of his life that you might live in the fullness of your individual God Self-awareness. Furthermore, you owe a debt of gratitude to the early devotees who did in fact call forth the flame with intense purity and devotion to the cause of mankind's freedom and therefore made possible the second phase of the dispensation whereby you and countless others have been given the knowledge of the violet flame in recent years.

Wherever you are, as you read my words you can begin to experience the marvelous action of the violet fire coursing through your veins, penetrating the layers of the physical temple—the bloodstream, the nervous system, the brain—pressing through the chakras, swirling through the etheric body, passing over the pages of the written record of your incarnations on earth. Line by line, letter by letter, the flame—intelligent, luminous, directed by the mind of God—sets free the energies, electron by electron, of all past misuses of the sacred fire. And thus not one jot or tittle of the law of karma shall pass until all be fulfilled[4] in the freedom of the violet fire.

If you would have the benefit of this miraculous energy, if you would be visited by the genie of the lamp of freedom, the Master Saint Germain himself, you have but to make the call. For the fiat of Almighty God has gone forth, and it is cosmic law: The call compels the answer! But the call is a very special call. It is not the demand of the human consciousness, but the command of your Real Self, your own true being, the mediator between the I AM Presence and the soul. Thus you declare:

"In the name of the Christ Self and in the name of the living God, I call forth the energies of the sacred fire from the altar within my heart. In the name of the I AM THAT I AM, I invoke the violet flame to blaze forth from the center of the threefold flame, from the white-fire core of my own I AM Presence, multiplied by the momentum of the blessed Ascended Master Saint Germain. I call forth that light to penetrate my soul and to activate my soul memory of freedom and the original blueprint of my soul's destiny. I call forth the violet transmuting flame to pass through my four lower bodies and through my soul consciousness to transmute the cause and core of all that is less than my Christ-perfection, all that is not in keeping with the will of God for my lifestream. So let it be done by the cloven tongues of the fire of the Holy Spirit [5] in fulfillment of the action of that sacred fire as above, so below. And I accept it done this hour in the full power of the living God who even now declares within my soul, 'I AM WHO I AM.'"

The violet flame comes forth from that aspect of the white light which is called the seventh ray. It is indeed the seventh-ray aspect of the Holy Spirit. Just as the sunlight passing through a prism is refracted into the rainbow of the seven color rays, so in the consciousness of the Holy Spirit the light of the Christ is refracted for mankind's use in the planes of Matter. Each of the seven rays is a concentrated action of the light of God having a specific color and frequency resulting in a specific action of the Christ in body, mind, and soul. We shall consider the other six aspects of the sacred fire as our course unfolds.*

Now let us examine what happens when the specific of the violet fire is applied to the recalcitrant conditions of the human consciousness. When, as an act of your free will, you make the call to the violet flame and you surrender these unwanted, untoward conditions into the flame, the fire instantaneously begins the work of breaking down particles of substance that are part of the mass accumulation of hundreds and even thousands of incarnations when in ignorance you allowed to register—through your consciousness, through your attention, thoughts and feelings, words and actions—all of the degrading conditions to which the human race is heir.

I trust that I need not enumerate the seemingly endless but altogether finite qualities of limitation thrust upon the ethers—projectiles of the carnal mind—that have filled the wide-open spaces between the electrons and the nuclei of the atoms with the densities of mankind's carnality. Believe it or not, this energy can be as hard as concrete or as sticky as molasses as it registers in all of the four lower bodies, causing mental recalcitrance, hardness of heart, a lack of

*See *The Chela and the Path* by El Morya, published by The Summit Lighthouse.

sensitivity to the needs of others and creating a dense mass that prevents the soul from receiving the delicate impartations of the Holy Spirit. So thick is the wall of mankind's density, of layer upon layer of their misuses of the sacred fire, that they don't even recognize the ascended masters as their liberators nor are they able to make contact with the blessed Christ Self, their own mediator of perfection who would confirm the reality of the ascended masters.

When the violet flame is invoked, it loosens the dense substance and passes through and transforms that darkness into light. Since every human condition is the perversion of a divine condition, line for line, measure for measure, the human consciousness is changed into the divine and the energy that was locked in pockets of mortality is freed to enter the sockets of immortality. And each time a measure of energy is freed, a measure of a man ascends to the plane of God-awareness.

As you begin to use the violet flame, you will experience feelings of joy, lightness, hope, and newness of life as though clouds of depression were being dissolved by the very sun of your own being. And the oppression of the very dark, dank energies of human bondage literally melts in the fervent heat of freedom's violet fires.

Lord Zadkiel, archangel of the seventh ray, made certain that the chelas of the new age would understand the joyousness of the flame, and so he called it the violet singing flame. Indeed, this flaming presence causes the very atoms and molecules of your being to "sing" as they resume their normal frequency and are therefore brought into "pitch" with the keynote of your own lifestream. This keynote is the sounding of the chord of your own I AM Presence. And when, by the action of the violet flame, you free the energies of your four lower bodies to respond to that chord, the wonderful world of the microcosm moves in harmony with the grand Macrocosm of your I AM Presence and causal body.

The violet flame forgives as it frees, consumes as it transmutes, clears the records of past karma (thus balancing your debts to life), equalizes the flow of energy between yourself and other lifestreams, and propels you into the arms of the living God. Day by day you are ascending higher and higher in the planes of consciousness of your Christ Self as you use the scrubbing action of the violet flame and feel how the very walls of your mental body are scoured. You can think of the action in your desire body as though your emotions were being dunked in a chemical solution of purple liquid which dissolves the dirt that has accumulated for decades about the latticework of your feeling world.

Every day in every way the violet flame flushes out and renews your body cells, the cells of your mind, and the globule of your soul, polishing the jewel of consciousness until it glistens in the sunlight, dazzling as a pure molecule of being offered upon the altar of the sacred fire as an offering that is fitting for the Lord—your gift to God and man. And what better gift is there than the gift of selfhood? In reality, this is all that you have to offer. And so when you use the violet flame, you are laying down the impoverished self, the lesser self, that the self that is real might act to increase the blessings of God's consciousness worlds without end.

I recommend that you use the violet flame in the name and in the flame of Saint Germain. And in his words I say to all who would be chelas of the will of God, *try.* For as the Master Alchemist has said, in the word "try" is the sacred formula of being: Theos = God; Rule = Law; You = Being; *Theos + Rule + You = God's Law Active as Principle within Your Being (TRY).*[6]

Let the energies of the violet flame unlock your true self even as they sweep away the encrustations of the synthetic self. Let the violet flame work in you the works of God.

Until we meet again in Darjeeling, I AM

El Morya

Exponent of the Freedom
of God's Will

19

The Violet Transmuting Flame

To All Devotees
of the Violet Flame's Perfection
I Address Myself:

Seldom do mankind realize the glorious wisdom of the mind of God that has contrived the violet transmuting flame in all of its cosmic unfolding glory. It is difficult for the world in its present state of development to fully comprehend from the level of the human consciousness or through the power of the human mind those momentous, invisible actions and activities of the sacred fires of God.

You are not dealing with a figment of your imagination when you deal with the violet transmuting flame. When you gaze at mass accumulations of vapor floating lazily in the sky and producing the constantly changing panorama of cloud capers, you are able to conceive that on the spur of the moment what seems a billowing froth of air may become a turbulence of unforeseen destruction.

When the average individual calls the violet transmuting flame into action, he does not have the power to perceive the dancing stream of electrons which perform on the stage of his consciousness, nor is he aware of the tremendous cosmic energy involved therein. Even some of you do not realize this great potential that transcends both time and space and produces in the now of your life's adventure a blessed action of transmutation or cosmic change that moves you a step forward on the Path. This is accomplished

as the flame consumes the negative storehouses
of energy that reside in your subconscious world
and produce those disquieting manifestations
which you have often lamented. Thus the flame
prepares the way through the divine leveling process for the erection in their place of the most
benign and constructive endeavors which your
heart may desire.

It is difficult for humanity to pray or even to
aspire to cosmic heights of thought and service
when there is no established precedent in the
forcefield of the individual mind to act as a
guideline for developing in man the quality of
asking for what he ought to ask. In this *Pearl* of
instruction I am setting forth before you the fact
that in reality there are in the subconscious world
of even the greatest of saints hidden chambers of
astral horror which require transmutation. In an
unguarded moment these can and often do break
forth upon the surface of being into a state of
alignment with the most vicious and destructive
negative forces on the planet.

Just as mankind who are wise seek a
catharsis in their physical as well as their
emotional body to purge them from residual
substance, so it is essential that they purify their
entire consciousness through calling into action
the blessed violet flame which focuses the
forgiving, transmuting power of God. Many
devotees, unbeknownst to themselves, succeed in
invoking the violet flame through the power of
intercessory prayer and do call forth those activities of the sacred fire of God which in the
West are usually termed the action of the Holy
Spirit and which in the East are related to the

destruction of all that is unreal and the purification of the veil of maya by Lord Shiva.

Always remember, beloved ones, that exposure to the divine flames or the invocation of spiritual power, wisdom, and love in your world can never alter or harm any part of your being that is a manifestation of universal perfection. All that can be exposed or brought down are the forcefields of human thought and feeling which reinforce the strongholds of Satan and the seeds of Lucifer in the individual mind and heart.

Let us take for example a manifestation of that which is often prevalent in orthodox churches: self-righteousness and the defense of that righteousness. The followers of various religions do not hesitate to level at one another the most vile accusations involving twists of human doctrine and justifications of their own pet version of the will of God. They fight and spat like feline creatures and cast out of the window of their lives gentle thoughts of forgiving love as well as the opportunity for increased understanding. Can you not see how silly this is for mankind who profess to do the will of God, to espouse the cause of brotherhood and the healing ministry of the Christ to allow themselves to enter into a frame of mind wherein they consider heaven itself unable to defend the living Truth?

Take great care, then, beloved ones, to hold yourselves in a sweet and childlike spirit of obedience to the will of God, to be not overly inclined to rush to the defense of Truth; for Truth is its own best defense—not that we do not appreciate loyalty, but we have an equal appreciation for good behavior.

Mankind's indoctrination with the Luciferian spirit of rebellion is no part of the instruction of the living God. The force of rebellion is chaotic and robs man of his peace. How glorious it is when mankind pursue the outworking of the harmony of inner spheres in their lives and in their associations with others. Then they are able to clear the way before their own advancement in life and to perceive the universal intent as it manifests perfection's die. Thus are stamped upon the human image those aspects of the Divine that carry man back to his own Eden of perfection, at the same time propelling him forward in those adroit manifestations of life that show forth the self-mastery of the adept.

From time to time we have actually toyed with the idea of developing in man greater power over the elements and over the manifestations of nature. We have thought in effect to teach the neophyte how to bend the will of the universe in such a manner as to give him greater mastery that he might hasten the victory of mankind. Whenever we have given serious consideration to this question, we have sought, as is our custom, the advice of the Karmic Board and of those universal intelligences who are beyond us in the cosmic evolutionary scale. And in every case we have been admonished to search the akashic records and perceive that mankind in their lack of understanding have always misused such power when it was given to them.

In the name of heaven, blessed ones, the record clearly shows that humanity have misused their spiritual powers and forfeited their adeptship in its embryonic state even when they had great spiritual knowledge. Hence we have asked that the consciousness of mankind should be satisfied—especially those who revere the will of God—with the development in themselves of the beauty of wisdom's ray so that there might take place, along with their spiritual development, an adherence to wisdom's ray right while their latent spiritual powers are literally exploding.

In the past many among mankind have sought to develop their spiritual powers long before they developed their spiritual wisdom. When people do this it becomes necessary for the Karmic Lords to fling them back upon the shores of life until such a time as they are able to follow the prescribed Path. Therefore, I urge you, one and all, not to overlook at any stage in your development the use of the violet transmuting flame. For through the flame much can be consumed upon the altar of being that will thereby be deprived of the opportunity of acting in your world. Embodied mankind will find, if they will take the time to experiment with this law, that they will be able to curb the manifestation of negative karma in their life by invoking the consuming power of the Holy Spirit in this most direct and specific application to man's needs that clears the way for the unfoldment of his latent spiritual powers.

By commending yourselves unto the Good Shepherd of Righteousness, by commending yourselves unto the laws of infinite perfection manifesting in your finite realms, you begin the process of correctly using the highest laws that are outworking perfection so beautifully in our sphere.

May I extend to you divine felicitations upon the Path even as I pray that you will ever keep open the doorways of mind and heart to the unfoldment of both the universal will and the universal purpose. Thus a God Star born in your heart as a miniature focus of the Great Central Sun will become the diamond-shining mind of God through the impartation of those points of awareness that are so closely identified with the cosmic compass of universal purpose.

I am striving with you for your development upon the pathway of devotion and service to the causes of the Brotherhood and the one Cause of God which we seek to glorify.

Devotedly, your servant

Sanctus Germanus

*Message to America
and the People of Earth*

Hail, Friends of Freedom!

Hail, light-bearers of the ages! Hail, O America! Hail, O earth! Hail to the freedom flame in every heart and in all life throughout cosmos!

I AM come to salute the light of the I AM THAT I AM within you and to give to you a vision to forge your God-identity. I AM the keeper of the flame of freedom for every nation. Saint Germain you have called me, and Uncle Sam. I AM he, and I AM here! I AM in the flame of the holy science and of that religion which is yours to claim as the sacred fire within your heart.

People of America, people of earth, hear the cry of the ascended hosts of light who are not very far removed from you, but who are your elder brothers and sisters on the Path who have kept for you the vision of freedom throughout all ages. Since the days of Lemuria and Atlantis, since the days of the coming of the Buddha and the Christ and the children of Israel who crossed the Red Sea and made their way through the wilderness land until the promise was fulfilled, so the hosts of the Lord have come through the teachers and prophets and messengers of the ages.

Think you then that God cannot also reveal himself in this day and age as he did before? Our God is indeed a consuming fire, and that fire is

the baptism of the Holy Ghost within you. And
this is the age of that baptism and of the coming
of the violet flame for your freedom from every
form of bondage over the mind, the soul, the
heart, and the being of man.

I AM here to claim freedom for man and
woman and child and for every heart on earth
that beats with the heart of Almighty God. I AM
with the people of the Soviet Union, of China, of
America, and Africa. I AM with the peoples who
are striving for that freedom which is the
discipline of liberty under the law of God and not
that license for the indulgence in the carnal mind.

Yes, I AM a follower of Christ. I AM a
sponsor of the Christ within you, and he too is
my Saviour. And thus the Lord Jesus with me
serves now to be with the hosts of the Lord the
open door for freedom in America and in every
nation. This is that open door which no man can
shut.

But I tell you, people of earth, it is up to you
to claim that freedom. For as ever before, the
fallen ones who have invaded the governments
and the economies of the nations are ever present as the spoilers to take from you your God-
ordained liberty. Therefore I say, *claim it* in the
name of the I AM THAT I AM! Claim it and be
then one with God the majority vote for freedom
on earth. For what is peace without freedom?—
this I ask you. And let every leader of every
nation ponder in his heart this day what is that
peace that has not the freedom to be or to
worship God as the Divine Self of every soul.

Yes, I come—a believer and a teacher of the
law of reincarnation. If it were not so I would

have told you. The law of the coming again and again of the soul is your cosmic justice. It is your opportunity to prove the law and to earn that salvation that is the ascension in the light. This is the goal of true religion. It is the binding of the soul to God in freedom. This is the great proof which our Lord Jesus Christ gave in his ascension on Bethany's hill. But it is yours also to claim and it is yours to claim for your nation, people of earth.

Understand, then, that this earth is intended to be governed by the souls of light. Therefore, souls of light, I speak to you this night. Take your place in government and stand for truth and stand for freedom! And this is the true and the only revolution that you can espouse. It is that cause of freedom whereby you understand that the goal and the calling of America and every true free nation is to lead mankind into that way of higher consciousness. It is a revolution of light that will allow all that is not aright on earth to be righted by the law of freedom and by that baptism of the sacred fire.

Understand, then, that it is movement to the great God Self within that is your salvation in this age, that all problems of the economy, the ecology, and the government can be resolved if you will take only ten minutes each day to go within and to find your own God Self, to meditate and to use the science of the spoken Word whereby you chant the mantra of the free: "I AM a being of violet fire—I AM the purity God desires!" This is my mantra which I give to you as your initiation into the Aquarian age. Will you not repeat it with me now? [Audience

gives mantra with Saint Germain:] "I AM a being
of violet fire—I AM the purity God desires."

When you use the name of God to claim the
I AM as God's being and beness within you, then
you have that claim to all which follows, and
therefore you can take the mantra of Jesus
Christ, "I AM the way, the truth, and the life,"
and you may participate in that glorious life that
he lived.

See, then, that the cycles turn, that as Christ
came to teach you that the Christ lives within
you, so I AM come to sponsor the nations that
each individual nation under God might find that
Christ is the center and the consciousness of that
sacred labor that it is the destiny of each free
nation to pursue. Let the nation, then, be the
identity of the collective Christ consciousness in
this age. Let individuality be found in the
Community of the Holy Spirit as nation by
nation the children of God on earth forge their
God-identity. Therefore I say to you, in the
name of the Lord, the Almighty One, the great
God of Freedom to the earth: *Forge your God-
identity!*

I bring to you now the energies of the sacred
heart of Jesus, the energies of the sacred heart of
Mary, and of my own heart's consecration to the
way of freedom. I bring to you the knowledge of
the sacred fire and the threefold flame that beats
your very own heart. The threefold flame is the
gift of life. It is your opportunity for Selfhood,
for reality. And it is your joint-heirship with the
Christ who proved himself to be the incarnation
of the Word as Father, Son, and Holy Spirit were

the heartbeat and the energy of his ministry.

Behold, then, the chart of your own I AM Presence which was revealed to Moses as the I AM THAT I AM. Behold the individualization of the God flame whereby you can claim oneness with the Most High. Behold, then, your own Christ principle, your own Christ Self, living as the Mediator and as the one who is able to forgive and to forgive and to forgive. Understand, then, that the Christ is one, the only begotten Son, and yet that Christ, that one, that light in Jesus, the true light that lighteth every man that cometh into the world, is the body of God that is fragmented and repeated again and again and again for every incoming soul.

And therefore the potential to be Christ is with you at the moment of your birth, at the moment when the Holy Spirit breathes the breath of life into your temple. In that hour you have once again the opportunity to know the Self as God, the I AM THAT I AM, and to know the Self as Christ. And the sacred fire that lives within you is the Holy Spirit. And when you meditate upon that flame as power, wisdom, and love, I tell you that flame will leap, it will burst forth and fill all the house, all of the temple of your being. And you will find the quickening of your sacred centers and of your consciousness and of life within life, and then you will feel the power of a cosmos surging through you, and then you will know how the few and then the many will go forth for the saving of the nations for Almighty God.

For we would that all nations and all peoples would come under the God-dominion of the

Christ. And therefore we serve—angelic beings, archangels, and Elohim. We serve to set mankind free. We serve to teach mankind the law of their own immortality. We serve only to free you to be all that God has vouchsafed to you through the great teachers of East and West who have come over the thousands of years of earth's evolutions.

Not all that was passed from Jesus Christ to the disciples has been recorded for your use. And therefore it is up to us to return to you, through our messenger, that sacred teaching of the Christ whereby you too can be free, whereby you can work the works of the apostles and those who are called to be representatives of the Lord.

I say to you, people of light, accept your mission of the ages! Accept your role as the ones who are the protectors of freedom on earth. This indeed is America's destiny—to teach a way of life that is a form of government whereby each threefold flame and every living soul may commune with God and out of that communion evolve one vote and cast that vote for freedom. So let it be that this understanding of the inner communion is the foundation of God-government of the people, by the people, and for the people that shall not perish from the earth[1] if this nation, America, shall rise again to her God-destiny in this age and shall forge that unity that is sponsored by the Archangel Michael who comes for the deliverance, who comes to unite you, and who comes with a message: "Remember, ye are brethren!"

Therefore let brethren unite for the glorious victory of the Christ, for the Second Coming of

Jesus and the coming again of the gracious Lord
Buddha, Lord of the World and giver of the
Flame of Life to all peoples. So let the understanding of the convergence of the teachings of
East and West be the forte of the God-identified
man. And let souls who love the flame of purity
now acquaint themselves with the flame of
Mother,[2] and let that Mother of Cosmos nourish
once again new life and the new birth.

O Mother Liberty,[3] raise your torch high
and welcome all souls of light to America and to
earth and reveal the Book of the Law and let it be
the Everlasting Gospel. So let the angel come and
let him deliver to the hearts of this people and
every people on earth the understanding of the
one true Source and that energy which is God
vouchsafed to every living soul.

I call, then, to the lost tribes of the house of
Israel: Come forth and claim your God-identity!
Come out of all of the nations and be free and be
the teachers of the ages and know the I AM
THAT I AM within the heart and know your
Real Self as the ever-living Christ.

So let the violet flame be the quality of
mercy that is not strained.[4] Let the violet flame
be invoked daily. Let your meditation be upon
the flame and the flame frequency which you will
find in the violet-flame color. This is my ray.
This is the ray of the Aquarian age. This is the
color of freedom itself. So let it beat within your
heart. Let it infire your heart. Let it instill you
with that love of the early patriots and of those
who forged that victory of freedom many
centuries ago in the heart of Europe, in that little
country of Switzerland where there burns yet a

threefold flame for all peoples to dip into and to use for the victory.

O Afra and sons and daughters of Afra,[5] I call you to the one law of the I AM THAT I AM. I call you now. Heed the word of the ascended masters and prove your freedom and demonstrate your freedom and your ability to be whole. I speak then to the black and the white and to those of every race. Each one of you has the opportunity to bring forth a great genius to this earth, but it must be done by individual application and soul worth. It must be the forging of your Self out of the energy that God has placed within your heart.

Now come forth. I send you love. Be free, then, of all of the past. Let the earth be washed by the waters of the living Word. Let the records of war on every continent, of hatred and prejudice and strife be dissolved now. For I AM Saint Germain, the sponsor of a new era of freedom. I sponsor America and every nation on earth where freedom is enshrined, and I sponsor every soul who will yet live to be free.

People of America, pray for those who are not free in every way and safeguard your heritage of freedom. For when you lose the right to be free by the subtle encroachments of the fallen ones, you will regret the hour that you were not vigilant upon the wall as watchmen of the Lord. And when the cry to that watchman, "What of the night?" will be sounded, I am counting on every American to be the watchman on the wall of the Lord and the wall of freedom. And when the cry is given forth, then, what will your answer be? I say let it be, "All is well!"

I salute you in the flame of my heart. I seal you in the flame of my heart. And I AM with you in Christ, in Buddha, unto the end of the cycle of this age. Amen. Amen. Amen.

Saint Germain

21

*Dynamic Decrees
by the Messengers*

"Thou shalt also decree a thing, and it shall be established unto thee: and the light shall shine upon thy ways."[1]

At the Last Supper when our Lord took bread and blessed it and brake it and gave it to the disciples, he pronounced a worded formula for the ritual of transubstantiation. He said of the bread, "Take, eat; this is my body" and of the wine, "Drink ye all of it; for this is my blood of the new covenant, which is poured out for you."[2] Through these words that have been recited in the Christian celebration of communion these two thousand years, Jesus Christ has transferred to his disciples the same essential energy—'the blood', *the Spirit,* and 'the body', *the Matter,* which he imparted to them the night before his crucifixion.

This transfer of light, energy, and consciousness from the ascended master to his unascended disciples, using the bread and the wine as the instrument of the blessing, is the means provided by the Master for his disciples to assimilate the momentum of his Christ consciousness, ultimately to become one with him, hence also to be that Christ. Through this ritual the positive and negative energies of his being, which we call the 'Alpha' and 'Omega' of Jesus

Christ,[3] are continually available to the true followers of God.

Numerous accounts of the saints who have
lived solely on communion with no other or very
little sustenance,[4] some while they received the
stigmata, prove that "man shall not live by bread
alone, but by every word that proceedeth out of
the mouth of God."[5] This 'Word' is the sacred
fire; in this case it takes the form of the *call* given
as blessing pronounced aloud by the pastor; it is
also the Word 'made flesh' once again in the
bread and wine as Jesus Christ personally answers the call by endowing that substance with
the vibration of his own light body (in the bread)
and light essence (in the wine).

Before the bread and wine are consecrated in
this ritual of the science of the spoken Word,
they have no intrinsic spiritual properties. After
the consecration, they have become the vessel for
Christ himself, the agent of the Holy Spirit. Now
by the alchemy of the Holy Ghost they *are* the
'sacred Eucharist'. As Jesus Christ in answer to
our call is able to endow this substance with the
flame of his life, so he is able to endow our very
souls and vehicles of consciousness (the physical,
mental, feeling, and memory bodies) with the
same light, energy, and consciousness of his life.
Indeed the Maha Chohan has said, "it was and is
and remains forever the purpose of God to imbue
his creation with his own Spirit."[6]

This capacity to endow life with the greater
flame of the Holy Ghost is the all-power of
heaven and earth[7] granted by God to his servant-
sons, the ascended masters. This transfer of
energy, the 'virtue' of their 'garment',[8] is actually

the gift of the light of their aura, called the electronic forcefield, or the Electronic Presence. It is given to those who raise up to the Great I AM the chalice of the self, forged by love and illumined obedience to God's will.

The gift of the ascended master's energy is that grace which comes as the reward for diligent effort on the path of good works (karma yoga), of devotion to God in the Personhood of the Trinity and the Mother (bhakti yoga), of study of the teachings of the Godhead through his emissaries (jnana yoga), and of the science of the Word and the sacred fire of the Holy Ghost (raja yoga). The ascended masters' consciousness— their attainment, their self-mastery—is always available to their chelas through their dynamic decrees. Decrees are the call which compels the answer—the Word made flesh: "I AM the living bread which came down from heaven."[9]

In the fourteenth century B.C., Joshua, "Moses' minister,"[10] was commanded by the Lord to compass the accursed city of Jericho with all his men of war and seven priests bearing seven trumpets before the ark of the covenant. They thus circumambulated the walled city once on each of six succeeding days. On the seventh day, when the priests blew their trumpets Joshua said unto the people, "Shout; for the Lord hath given you the city." With that thundering word it is recorded that "the wall fell down flat."[11] Yes, dynamic decrees!

Unto the prophet Isaiah "saith the Lord, the Holy One of Israel, and his Maker, Ask me of things to come concerning my sons,..." This is communication, prayer—walking and talking with God as Friend. Prayer is an important and necessary conversation with God which includes our questioning and his answering. But the Lord did not stop there. He went on to say, "and concerning the work of my hands *command ye me.*"[12] With these words God introduced to Isaiah the science of the spoken Word. *The command.*

God is actually telling us to *command* him. But concerning what? "Concerning the work of my hands," concerning the creation and its alchemical components—light, energy, and consciousness. Concerning the plane of action—Matter, time and space, and our three-dimensional opportunity to exercise the gift of free will, to demonstrate God's laws, and to return to the plane of First Cause, Spirit.

The command is the Word described as "a sharp sword" that goeth forth out of the mouth of the Faithful and True to smite the nations.[13] It is the sacred fire that proceedeth out of the mouth of "the two witnesses" to devour their enemies.[14] It is the mystical power of the saints who overcome "the dragon" (the illusion of the not-self) "by the blood of the Lamb" (the light, energy, and consciousness of the Christ) "and by the *word* of their testimony" (by their dynamic decrees).[15] Of this command the Lord declares to Isaiah, "So shall my Word be that goeth forth out of my mouth: it shall not return unto me void, but it shall accomplish that which I please, and it shall prosper in the thing whereto I sent it."[16]

Jesus Christ demonstrated the science of the spoken Word as the key to self-mastery through conscious cooperation with God. Let us further consider this action of the Word by which he performed his 'miraculous' works.

Paul testifies of Jesus Christ "upholding all things by the Word of his power."[17] Indeed it is written that he "rebuked the wind, and said unto the sea, Peace, be still. And the wind ceased, and there was a great calm."[18] He commanded the unclean spirits to go out of the Gadarene demoniac. He gave them leave *by the authority of his Word* and they entered into the swine.[19]

When Lazarus was already four days in the grave, Jesus, thanking the Father "that thou hast heard me,"[20] nevertheless "cried with a loud voice, Lazarus, come forth!"[21] To the woman who touched his garment Jesus said, "Daughter, thy faith hath made thee whole; go in peace, and be whole of thy plague."[22] And to Jairus' daughter, "Damsel, I say unto thee, arise."[23] To the sick of the palsy he commanded, "Son, thy sins be forgiven thee,"[24] to Levi, "Follow me,"[25] and to the man with the withered hand, "Stand forth....Stretch forth thine hand."[26] In each case they were made whole—their very souls were realigned with the Spirit of God by the dynamism of his voice, by the command of his Christ Presence.

This is the 'Command ye me!' of Jesus Christ in action, demonstrating the science of the spoken Word which the Lord God intended all of his sons and daughters to exercise—wherefore he gave to them through his servant Moses his very own name, I AM THAT I AM.[27] The name of the Lord, called by mystics the Tetragrammaton, unlocks the power, the energy, the consciousness by which all things are made through the Word.[28]

The name is more than a name. It is the Flaming One, the Presence of God the Father who has individualized himself as pulsating spheres within spheres, the Origin of the embodied soul. (See Chart facing p. 200.) The name of God, I AM, when spoken releases the energy locked in the nucleus of the Permanent Atom of Self (the 'I AM' Presence, a term used interchangeably with the I AM THAT I AM). Whatever you affirm following that statement *must* cycle into manifestation, descending from the plane of the Father, to the plane of the Son, the individual Christ Self, to the plane of the soul where it is released through the heart center.

Jesus had tremendous power in his words, and he drew that power from the threefold flame—Father, Son, and Holy Spirit—burning on the altar of his heart. Many disciples of Christ have beheld that sacred heart of Jesus as well as the immaculate heart of Mary. To the Hindus it is *Anāhata,* the heart *chakra.* To all who pray and meditate both East and West, the heart is the center of that burning love of God which the disciples knew when they met their Lord on the road to Emmaus.[29]

"I AM the resurrection, and the life."[30] This is a precise formula of the Word given to Jesus Christ by Lord Maitreya when he journeyed to the retreats of the Himalayan brotherhood between the ages of twelve and thirty in preparation for his Galilean ministry. Even now as you give this affirmation in full voice, you immediately experience the resurrection and the life of the God flame within because you are speaking the name of God, I AM, through the

Word transferred to you by Jesus Christ through
your own Christ Self.

Jesus Christ, the Son of God, the incarnation of the Word, had the authority of the
Father to give this power not only to the
apostles—who used it to cast out devils and heal
the sick[31] —but also to as many as received him
that believe on his name.[32] This authority he yet
retains, and to his disciples who are one with him
in the vibration of the Word he entrusts the
power of the spoken Word and the understanding of its science.

Having received all power in heaven and in
earth[33] by the utter giving of the self to the will of
the Father, the Avatar of the Piscean age, the
Great Guru of the Word, the Beloved, transferred to his chelas this selfsame power. He
commanded them to use it to baptize and to
teach the nations "to observe all things whatsoever I have commanded you."[34] And he taught
them the infallible law of the Trinity:

"Whatsoever command ye give in the name
of the Father, and of the Son, and of the Holy
Ghost it shall be multiplied unto you by the
'power of the three times three'. If your command be of God, good shall follow; but if it be
evil, then woe to you, for it shall also be multiplied unto you. Even so, neither God nor his
Great Law will be mocked. Whatsoever a man
soweth, that shall he also reap."[35]

Our Saviour knew the supreme import of
teaching his disciples the science of the name of
God. In his final prayer of intercession to the
Father, made just before he entered the Garden
of Gethsemane, he conversed with the All-

Loving One concerning his work on earth and the instruction which he had given to the disciples whom the Father had given him—the vital instruction on the name of God and its power whereby he himself would demonstrate the law of eternal life: "I have manifested thy *name* unto the men which thou gavest me out of the world...Holy Father, keep through thine own *name* those whom thou hast given me, that they may be one, as we are...while I was with them in the world, I kept them in thy *name*...I have declared unto them thy *name*, and will declare it: that the love wherewith thou hast loved me may be in them, and I in them."[36] Let us take note that the Greek origin of *name* in these four instances is *onoma* 'name, authority, character'.

To understand dynamic decrees we must know what, indeed, is this name of the Lord whereby men may be saved when they call upon it.[37] Through Moses, God had given his people the I AM THAT I AM saying, "This is my name for ever, and this is my memorial unto all generations."[38] Nowhere else in the entire Judeo-Christian dispensation, whether in Old or New Testament or in the Apocrypha, do we find a record of the Lord God himself declaring his name in such a forthright and final manner. Now, Jesus avowedly came to fulfill the law and the prophets.[39] When teaching the name of God, he would give no other but that which God himself had already given through his prophet and lawgiver. Unquestionably, the name of God which Jesus, the obedient servant-son, taught the apostles was I AM THAT I AM—because this was the name God wanted his people to have—a memorial to *all* generations. None are excluded from the power of his name or the science of the Word.

While Jesus taught that those who would work the works of God must believe on him whom he hath sent[40] (the Word incarnate in Jesus Christ and the individual Christ Self of the sons and daughters of God), his own great work was to transfer the law of the sacred fire to his disciples—the same fire of the I AM Presence that burned in the bush before Moses.[41] The Master himself was the unbroken thread of contact with Mt. Sinai, the Holy of Holies, where God revealed for all time and space the Law of the One.

This living Presence of God, this Great I AM, is the great gift of the gurus which has descended from Abraham through the prophets unto the seed of the Virgin.[42] The transfer of the authority of Jesus Christ to his apostles is in the understanding that the invocation of the name of God, I AM THAT I AM, through the Word (Logos) unlocks God's power, his authority, the very essence of his nature (his character) *when it is given in the vibration of perfect love.*

In the same prayer Jesus said to the Father, "I have given them thy *Word*....Sanctify them through thy truth: thy *Word* is truth."[43] He spoke of the *Logos.* He spoke of himself. He spoke of all who would follow him in this dispensation of the incarnate Word. Here we find the same Greek origin of the 'Word' John used when he wrote, "In the beginning was the Word, and the Word was with God, and the Word was

God. The same was in the beginning with God. All things were made by him [the Word]; and without him [the Word] was not any thing made that was made."[44]

This Logos[45] is the Second Person of the Trinity which was incarnate in Jesus. This Logos which was and is with God is the eternal life[46] which Jesus Christ has the power to give to those whom God has given him. It is God's desire and the purpose to which he sent his Son into the world[47] that we should become the sons of God (the Christs of God) hence, like unto him, the Logos incarnate, his life eternal made manifest both now (in Matter) and forever (in Spirit).

The reason Jesus gave his magnificent prayer offering 'The Hour Is Come' recorded in Chapter 17 of the Gospel of John was that he knew the requirement of the Great Law. He would not be permitted to enter Gethsemane or to take the initiation of the crucifixion until he had imparted to his disciples the great mystery of the name of God, I AM THAT I AM, (the power to create in heaven and in earth, "the power over all flesh")[48] and the equally great mystery of the Word of God (the Logos whereby the creation is made manifest both in Spirit and in Matter). This teaching was and is the indispensable oneness of Father and Son which Jesus exemplified every day of his life.

That all might *know* this oneness was the real purpose of his mission. "And this is life eternal, that they might *know* thee the only true God, and Jesus Christ, whom thou hast sent."[49] It is thus the *knowledge* of the Law of the One, of the soul in Christ and of the Christ in God, which enables us to consciously partake of the accelerating Light of the Logos—that life eternal. To his own he defined precisely the relationship of the soul to God, individualized as the I AM Presence, and to Jesus Christ, individualized in the Christ Self.

Without this specific knowledge we could not follow him in the regeneration. Thus Jesus dutifully, joyfully, reports to the Father that his work is accomplished. "Father, the hour is come; glorify thy Son, that thy Son also may glorify thee."[50] Now he takes up his cross and bears the weight of our personal and planetary karma, the sins of the world for a time and a space, that we may follow him all the way Home through the regeneration of the Word.

Thus the science of the Word is the creative energy that sets in motion the creation of both God and man. It is the culmination in love of scientific prayer and scientific meditation that can manifest as good works if man and woman will it so.

All that God experiences is the result of his Word. All that man experiences is the result of his use or abuse of the same creative Word. So powerful is the energy of the Holy Spirit—the actual energy that is qualified in each exercise of the spoken Word—that Jesus warned: "But he that shall blaspheme against the Holy Ghost hath never forgiveness [so long as he continues to blaspheme], but is in danger of eternal damnation."[51]

The energy of the Holy Spirit, called the sacred fire by the ascended masters, is little understood by the masses of the people. Its

misuse results in insanity and demon possession
and is marked by sexual perversions, promis-
cuity, and the denial of the laws of God in daily
practice as well as the denial of the person of God
embodied in his sons and daughters.

This blasphemy against the Holy Ghost is
spoken of by Daniel the Prophet as the abom-
ination of desolation, standing in the holy place
where it ought not.[52] The holy place is the temple of the living God, man's own body and
soul.[53] The desecration of this temple comes
about through all uncleanness of spirit[54]—dis-
honesty, gossip, hatred, self-indulgence, con-
demnation, belittlement, lust, psychedelic drugs,
marijuana, rock music, anger against God, rebellion against his laws, all forms of immorality
and betrayal of the honor of God and the life of
his servant-sons.

The reconsecration of the temple is made
possible by the very same energy, the sacred fire
of the Holy Ghost, when it is invoked through
the science of the spoken Word in the name of
God, I AM THAT I AM, and his Son Jesus
Christ. Through the law of grace and forgiveness
the temple of man's consciousness, his heart and
mind and soul, are cleansed by the purifying
agency of the Holy Spirit. Many who have
witnessed this fiery baptism[55] within their souls
have actually seen and felt the violet flame
coming into their temple to purge them of their
sin and the sense of struggle. They have experienced the healing of their minds of the intent
to sin, of inordinate desire, and impure motive.

The suffering yet experienced by embodied
mankind is proof not of an unjust God; on the

contrary, it illustrates the consistency of a loving God who desires to bestow upon his children the gift of his own Selfhood. It reveals a God consistently obedient to his own laws, not playing favorites as Peter said, "Of a truth I perceive that God is no respecter of persons: But in every nation he that feareth him [his name], and worketh righteousness [exerciseth the 'right use' of the law of his Logos], is accepted with him."[56] Thus God—exacting from all the same obedience, love, and humility before the indwelling Christ and the incarnate Word—rewards each according to his words and his work. "By thy words thou shalt be justified, and by thy words thou shalt be condemned. . . . And, behold, I come quickly; and my reward is with me, to give every man according as his work shall be."[57]

This is the law of *karma*. Simply put, it is the law of individual accountability whereby each one must give an accounting for his free-will use of the energy of the Holy Ghost—by his words and by his work. It is the wisdom of the Great Guru to return over and over again to his disciples the fruits of their consciousness until finally they should bend the knee and confess that he alone is Lord. This path of God's initiation of your soul is ongoing. Lifetime after lifetime, we return to the plane of existence where we have qualified God's light, energy, and consciousness with good or evil, there to experience the consequences of our actions (our *karma*), ultimately to decide to be only God—to live and move and have our being in him simply because we *are* his offspring.[58]

Now as it is prophesied in the Book of Revelation, this true teaching of Jesus Christ, concerning the name of God, his Word, and the energy of the Holy Ghost given to his disciples during the forty days following his resurrection, is given to all of God's children, "to every nation and kindred and tongue and people." It is the new testament,[59] the new covenant,[60] the Everlasting Gospel,[61] and the new song sung by the 144,000 before the Lamb (the individual Christ Self) on Mount Zion (in the mountain of God, the plane of the I AM THAT I AM).[62]

Truly the gift of the violet flame is the Promised Comforter[63] extended through the hand of God's emissary in the Aquarian age, Saint Germain. Truly it is the fulfillment of the prophecy of God's own law of transmutation "Though your sins be as scarlet, they shall be as white as snow; though they be red like crimson, they shall be as wool."[64] The violet flame is the specific of the Holy Spirit, the antidote, that dissolves the unrighteous works of man and restores his soul to righteousness and the lawful desire to be God in action.

The violet flame does not destroy, for the law is precise: God's energy is neither created nor destroyed. The violet flame *changes* the water into wine.[65] It strips atoms and molecules of the dense overlay of human imperfection and restores the natural divine perfection of the soul and its original desire to be whole. It dissolves the encrustations of vanity, illusion, the delusions of the pseudo self, and even the laws of old age and death. It is the elixir of life, the fountain of youth, the laughter of angels. Its buoyant

strength and zestful joy make mockery of the
devil and hell. Yes, even the demons "also
believe, and tremble"[66] before its all-consuming
conflagration. Why, in its wake all that is left is
all that is real in you and in God!

Peter spoke of the Lord God—the Law of
the Sacred Fire—"coming as a thief in the night,"
coming, that is, to strip the children of God
of the energy which they have misused, misqualified, in Matter. (The term *night* symbol-
izes the time/space continuum in Matter.) In that
hour of the Lord's coming, Peter foresaw that
"the heavens shall pass away with a great noise,
and the elements shall melt with fervent heat, the
earth also and the works that are therein shall be
burned up."[67] This is not a day to be feared, but
one to be anticipated with all rejoicing and glory
to God. The terms 'heaven' and 'earth' refer to
planes of consciousness, Spirit and Matter, that
coexist right within the being of God's children.

Peter had an apocalyptic vision of the
chemicalization that would occur within his own
consciousness as the violet flame would descend
"with the Holy Ghost and with fire"[68] to baptize
him into that self-awareness in God's kingdom
(i.e., God's consciousness) that John also beheld
as the "new heaven and the new earth."[69] Peter
saw and taught that the only preparation for this
"day of the Lord"[70] was (1) "all holy conversation"—meaning the correct use of the science
of the spoken Word not only in prayer, meditation, and dynamic decrees, but also in the
hour-to-hour uses of the spoken Word in conversation, in all verbal and written communication,
for both carry the energy of the Holy Ghost for

blessing (harmony) or bane (discord); and (2) "godliness" meaning good works—working the works of God and in all things giving him the full credit for each accomplishment—"I can of mine own self do nothing, it is the Father in me who doeth the work."[71] This acknowledgment day by day is the glory and honor due his name.

Gautama Buddha defined "godliness" as the Eightfold Path of right knowledge, right aspiration, right speech, right behavior, right livelihood, right effort, right mindfulness, right absorption. And in this *'Be-attitude'*—the blessed attitude of Be-ness, of being God—the paths of East and West are one. Thus Peter, commending Christ's followers to "all holy conversation" and "godliness," was rapturously endued with this singular vision of the Holy Spirit now upon us in the dispensation of the violet flame. My beloved, he was "looking for and hasting unto the coming of the day of God, wherein the heavens being on fire shall be dissolved, and the elements shall melt with fervent heat."[72]

Now as you begin to invoke the blessed sacred fire of the Holy Spirit into your temple, you can look for and hasten this great and notable day[73] of the Lord's transformation, i.e., transmutation, in your body, soul, heart, and mind. For all of these, your very identity, are God's—God's energy and his life which he has given to you whereby your consciousness may be fruitful in Christ, and multiply his grace, and replenish the earth with blessing and peace, and subdue it, and have dominion over it[74] by the power of his Word.

Fully aware of the alchemy of the coming

age Djwal Kul, Guru of Tibet, has said: "For the daily balancing of karma and the transmutation of decadent energies of the past, for the spiritual irrigation of the chakras with the flowing Word of Life, for the filling of the aura with light, for the expansion and the holding of the expansion of the aura, there is no system, ancient or modern, that can replace the science of the spoken Word revealed by Lord Maitreya, demonstrated by the messengers, and prescribed by the chohans of the rays for their chelas who would make the most rapid advances on the path to self-mastery."[75]

Now take the violet flame—in the following dynamic decrees dictated to us by the Holy Spirit of the ascended masters—and liberate atoms, cells, and electrons in every plane of your heaven and your earth. Let the Lord's energies which you have locked in human habit patterns of misunderstanding be unlocked by the divine habit pattern of understanding God's laws governing man's efficient use of the sacred fire. Let the Lord's energy, captive to the human will, now be captive to the divine will. Let it come forth in obedience to the grand design which we now invoke as the blueprint of our earth and her evolutions. Let his light, energy, and consciousness in us and through us work a work of wonder as we stand on the threshold of the age of Aquarius.[76] Truly let us *let* God's kingdom come on earth as it is in heaven[77] through the science of the spoken Word that has echoed through the Voice of Elohim from the beginning of "let there be light!" unto the ending "and there was light!"[78]

Through the 'Command ye me' of the Word

of God *within you,* in the full alchemy of the violet flame, you can experience the new birth in Christ and the invigorating infilling of the Holy Spirit. By the violet flame, you can cleanse the temple that it might be a fitting habitation for your God. And he will surely come with the rushing of a mighty wind[79] and the sound of many waters.[80] He will surely come in the fullness of his Word.

Even so come quickly, Lord Jesus.[81]

I AM the Violet Flame

In the name of the beloved mighty victorious Presence of God, I AM in me, and my very own beloved Holy Christ Self, I call to beloved Alpha and Omega in the heart of God in our Great Central Sun and to the heart of the Saviour Jesus Christ and the servant-sons of God who are with him in heaven—beloved Saint Germain, beloved Portia, beloved Archangel Zadkiel, beloved Holy Amethyst, beloved mighty Arcturus and Victoria, beloved Kuan Yin, Goddess of Mercy, beloved Oromasis and Diana, beloved Mother Mary, beloved Omri-Tas, Ruler of the Violet Planet, beloved Great Karmic Board, beloved Lanello, the entire Spirit of the Great White Brotherhood and the World Mother; elemental life—fire, air, water, and earth! to expand the violet flame within my heart, purify my four lower bodies, transmute all misqualified energy I have ever imposed upon life, and blaze mercy's healing ray throughout the earth, the elementals, and all mankind and answer this my call infinitely, presently, and forever:

> I AM the violet flame
>   In action in me now
> I AM the violet flame
>   To light alone I bow
> I AM the violet flame
>   In mighty cosmic power
> I AM the light of God
>   Shining every hour
> I AM the violet flame
>   Blazing like a sun
> I AM God's sacred power
>   Freeing every one

And in full faith I consciously accept this manifest, manifest, manifest (3x) right here and now with full power, eternally sustained, all-powerfully active, ever expanding, and world enfolding until all are wholly ascended in the light and free! Beloved I AM, beloved I AM, beloved I AM!

Radiant Spiral Violet Flame

In the name of the beloved mighty victorious Presence of God, I AM in me, my very own beloved Holy Christ Self, I call to the heart of the Saviour Jesus Christ and the servant-sons of God who are with him in heaven—beloved Lanello, the entire Spirit of the Great White Brotherhood and the World Mother; elemental life—fire, air, water, and earth!

> Radiant spiral violet flame,
>   Descend, now blaze through me;
> Radiant spiral violet flame,
>   Set free, set free, set free!
>
> Radiant violet flame, O come,
>   Drive and blaze thy light through me;
> Radiant violet flame, O come,
>   Reveal God's power for all to see;
> Radiant violet flame, O come,
>   Awake the earth and set it free.
>
> Radiance of the violet flame,
>   Explode and boil through me;
> Radiance of the violet flame,
>   Expand for all to see;
> Radiance of the violet flame,
>   Establish mercy's outpost here;
> Radiance of the violet flame,
>   Come, transmute now all fear.

And in full faith I consciously accept this manifest, manifest, manifest (3x) right here and now with full power, eternally sustained, all-powerfully active, ever expanding, and world enfolding until all are wholly ascended in the light and free! Beloved I AM, beloved I AM, beloved I AM!

The Law of Forgiveness

Beloved mighty victorious Presence of God, I AM in me, beloved Holy Christ Self, beloved Heavenly Father, I call to the heart of the Saviour Jesus Christ and the servant-sons of God who are with him in heaven— beloved Great Karmic Board, beloved Kuan Yin, Goddess of Mercy, beloved Lanello, the entire Spirit of the Great White Brotherhood and the World Mother; elemental life—fire, air, water, and earth! In the name and by the power of the Presence of God which I AM and by the magnetic power of the sacred fire vested in me, I call upon the law of forgiveness and the violet transmuting flame for each transgression of thy law, each departure from thy sacred covenants. Restore in me the Christ mind, forgive my wrongs and unjust ways, make me obedient to thy code, let me walk humbly with thee all my days. In the name of the Father, the Mother, the Son, and the Holy Spirit, I decree for all whom I have ever wronged and for all who have ever wronged me:

> Violet fire,* enfold us!   (3x)
> Violet fire, hold us!   (3x)
> Violet fire, set us free!   (3x)
> *"Mercy's flame" or "purple flame" may be used here.

I AM, I AM, I AM surrounded by
    a pillar of violet flame,*
I AM, I AM, I AM abounding in
    pure love for God's great name,
I AM, I AM, I AM complete
    by thy pattern of perfection so fair,
I AM, I AM, I AM God's radiant flame
    of love gently falling through the air.

*"Mercy's flame" or "purple flame" may be used for "violet flame"

> Fall on us!   (3x)
> Blaze through us!   (3x)
> Saturate us!   (3x)

And in full faith . . .

O Saint Germain, Send Violet Flame

Beloved mighty victorious Presence of God, I AM in me, thou immortal unfed flame of Christ-love within my heart, Holy Christ Selves of all mankind, I call to the heart of the Saviour Jesus Christ and the servant-sons of God who are with him in heaven—beloved Ascended Master Saint Germain, beloved Mother Mary, the beloved Maha Chohan, Archangel Zadkiel, Prince Oromasis, all great beings, powers, and activities of light serving the violet transmuting flame, beloved Lanello, the entire Spirit of the Great White Brotherhood and the World Mother; elemental life—fire, air, water, and earth!

In the name and by the power of the Presence of God which I AM and by the magnetic power of the sacred fire vested in me, I invoke the mighty presence and power of your full-gathered momentum of service to the light of God that never fails, and I command that it be directed throughout my entire consciousness, being, and world, through my affairs, the activities of The Summit Lighthouse, and all ascended-master activities, worlds without end. In thy name, O God, I decree:

1. O Saint Germain, send violet flame,
   Sweep it through my very core;
   Bless'd Zadkiel, Oromasis,
   Expand and intensify more and more.

Refrain:
   Right now blaze through and saturate,
   Right now expand and penetrate;
   Right now set free, God's mind to be,
   Right now and for eternity.

2. I AM in the flame and there I stand,
   I AM in the center of God's hand;
   I AM filled and thrilled by violet hue,
   I AM wholly flooded through and through.

(Continued)

3. I AM God's flame within my soul,
   I AM God's flashing beacon goal;
   I AM, I AM the sacred fire
   I feel the flow of joy inspire.

4. The consciousness of God in me
   Does raise me to the Christ I see.
   Descending now in violet flame,
   I see him come fore'er to reign.

5. O Jesus, send thy violet flame,
   Sanctify my very core;
   Blessed Mary, in God's name,
   Expand and intensify more and more.

6. O mighty I AM, send violet flame,
   Purify my very core;
   Maha Chohan, thou holy one,
   Expand, expand God's lovely sun.

Coda:*
   He takes me by the hand to say,
   I love thy soul each blessed day;
   O rise with me into the air
   Where blossoms freedom from all care;
   As violet flame keeps blazing through,
   I know that I'll ascend with you.

   *To be given at the end of the decree.

And in full faith I consciously accept this manifest, manifest, manifest (3x) right here and now with full power, eternally sustained, all-powerfully active, ever expanding, and world enfolding until all are wholly ascended in the light and free! Beloved I AM, beloved I AM, beloved I AM!

Arcturus, Blessed Being Bright

Beloved mighty victorious Presence of God, I AM in me, thou immortal unfed flame of Christ-love burning within my heart, Holy Christ Selves of all mankind, I call to the heart of the Saviour Jesus Christ and the servant-sons of God who are with him in heaven—beloved mighty Elohim Arcturus and Victoria, all great beings, powers, and activities of light serving the violet flame, beloved Lanello, the entire Spirit of the Great White Brotherhood and the World Mother; elemental life—fire, air, water, and earth!

In the name and by the magnetic power of the Presence of God which I AM and by the magnetic power of the sacred fire vested in me, I invoke the mighty presence and power of your full-gathered momentum of service to the light of God that never fails, and I command that it be directed throughout all mankind, elemental life, and the angelic hosts serving earth's evolutions. Blaze thy dazzling light of a thousand suns throughout the earth and transmute all that is not of the light into the God-victorious, light all-glorious, flaming Jesus Christ perfection. In thy name, O God, I decree:

1. O Arcturus, blessed being bright,
   Flood, flood, flood our world with light;
   Bring forth perfection everywhere,
   Hear, O hear our earnest prayer.

   Refrain:
   Charge us with thy violet flame,
   Charge, O charge us in God's name;
   Anchor in us all secure,
   Cosmic radiance, make us pure.

2. O Arcturus, blessed Elohim,
   Let thy light all through us stream;
   Complement our souls with love
   From thy stronghold up above.

(Continued)

3. O Arcturus, violet flame's great master,
   Keep us safe from all disaster;
   Secure us in the cosmic stream,
   Help expand God's loving dream.

4. O Arcturus, dearest lord of might,
   By thy star radiance beaming bright,
   Fill us with thy cosmic light,
   Raise, O raise us to thy height.

And in full faith...

O Violet Flame, Come, Violet Flame!

In the name of the beloved mighty victorious
Presence of God, I AM in me, my very own beloved
Holy Christ Self, I call to the heart of the Saviour Jesus
Christ and the servant-sons of God who are with him in
heaven—beloved Lanello, the entire Spirit of the Great
White Brotherhood and the World Mother; elemental
life—fire, air, water, and earth!

O violet flame, come, violet flame,
   Now blaze and blaze and blaze!
O violet flame, come, violet flame,
   To raise and raise and raise!

(Repeat verse between the following endings:)

1. The earth and all thereon   (3x)

2. The children and their teachers   (3x)

3. The plants and elemental creatures   (3x)

4. The air, the sea, the land   (3x)

5. Make all to understand   (3x)

6. Bless all by Omri-Tas' hand   (3x)

7. I AM, I AM, I AM the fullness of God's
   plan fulfilled right now and forever   (3x)

And in full faith...

Fiat for Freedom's Holy Light
by Saint Germain

(These fiats may be given 33 times each for the acceleration of the momentum
of God-freedom within the temple of being.)

Mighty cosmic light,
My own I AM Presence bright,
  Proclaim freedom everywhere;
In order and by God-control
I AM making all things whole!

Mighty cosmic light,
Stop the lawless hordes of night,
  Proclaim freedom everywhere;
In justice and in service true
I AM coming, God, to you!

Mighty cosmic light,
I AM law's prevailing might,
  Proclaim freedom everywhere;
In magnifying all good will
I AM freedom living still!

Mighty cosmic light,
Now make all things right,
  Proclaim freedom everywhere;
In love's victory all shall go,
I AM the wisdom all shall know!

I AM freedom's holy light
  Nevermore despairing,
I AM freedom's holy light
  Evermore I'm sharing.
Freedom, freedom, freedom,
  Expand, expand, expand!
  I AM, I AM, I AM,
Forevermore I AM freedom!

More Violet Fire
A Fiat by Hilarion

Lovely God Presence, I AM in me,
Hear me now I do decree:
Bring to pass each blessing for which I call
Upon the Holy Christ Self of each and all.

Let violet fire of freedom roll
Round the world to make all whole;
Saturate the earth and its people, too,
With increasing Christ-radiance shining through.

I AM this action from God above,
Sustained by the hand of heaven's love,
Transmuting the causes of discord here,
Removing the cores so that none do fear.

I AM, I AM, I AM
The full power of freedom's love
Raising all earth to heaven above.
Violet fire now blazing bright,
In living beauty is God's own light

Which right now and forever
Sets the world, myself, and all life
Eternally free in ascended-master perfection.
Almighty I AM, almighty I AM, almighty I AM!

YOUR DIVINE SELF

Chart of Your Divine Self

There are three figures represented in the chart, which we will refer to as the upper figure, the middle figure, and the lower figure. The upper figure is the I AM Presence, the I AM THAT I AM, God individualized for every son and daughter of God. The Divine Monad consists of the I AM Presence surrounded by the spheres (rings of color, of light) which comprise the causal body.

This is the body of First Cause that contains within it man's "treasure laid up in heaven"— perfect works, perfect thoughts and feelings, perfect words—energies that have ascended from the plane of action in time and space as the result of man's correct exercise of free will and his correct qualification of the stream of life that issues forth from the heart of the Presence and descends to the level of the Christ Self.

The middle figure in the chart is the mediator between God and man, called the Christ Self, the Real Self, or the Christ consciousness. It has also been referred to as the Higher Mental Body or Higher Consciousness. The Christ Self overshadows the lower self, which consists of the soul evolving through the four planes of Matter in the four lower bodies corresponding to the planes of fire, air, water, and earth; that is, the etheric body, the mental body, the emotional body, the physical body.

The three figures of the chart correspond to the Trinity of Father (the upper figure), Son (the middle figure), and Holy Spirit. The lower figure is intended to become the temple for the Holy Spirit which is indicated in the enfolding violet-flame action of the sacred fire. The lower figure corresponds to you as a disciple on the Path.

Your soul is the nonpermanent aspect of being which is made permanent through the ritual of the ascension. The ascension is the process whereby the soul, having balanced his karma and fulfilled his divine plan, merges first with the Christ consciousness and then with the living Presence of the I AM THAT I AM. Once the ascension has taken place, the soul, the corruptible aspect of being, becomes the incorruptible one, a permanent atom in the body of God. The chart of your Divine Self is therefore a diagram of yourself—past, present, and future.

The lower figure represents mankind evolving in the planes of Matter. This is how you should visualize yourself standing in the violet flame, which you invoke in the name of the I AM Presence and in the name of your Christ Self in order to purify your four lower bodies in preparation for the ritual of the alchemical marriage— your soul's union with the Lamb as the bride of Christ.

The lower figure is surrounded by a tube of light, which is projected from the heart of the I AM Presence in answer to your call. It is a field of fiery protection sustained in Spirit and in Matter for the sealing of the individuality of the disciple. The threefold flame within the heart is the spark of life projected from the I AM Presence through the Christ Self and anchored in the etheric planes in the heart chakra for the purpose of the soul's evolution in Matter. Also called the Christ flame, the threefold flame is the spark of man's divinity, his potential for Godhood.

The crystal cord is the stream of light that descends from the heart of the I AM Presence through the Christ Self, thence to the four lower bodies to sustain the soul's vehicles of expression in time and space. It is over this cord that the energy of the Presence flows, entering the being of man at the top of the head and providing the energy for the pulsation of the threefold flame and the physical heartbeat.

When a round of the soul's incarnation in Matter-form is complete, the I AM Presence withdraws the crystal cord, the threefold flame returns to the level of the Christ, and the energies of the four lower bodies return to their respective planes.

The dove of the Holy Spirit descending from the heart of the Father is shown just above the head of the Christ. When the individual man, as the lower figure, puts on and becomes the Christ consciousness as Jesus did, the descent of the Holy Spirit takes place and the words of the Father, the I AM Presence, are spoken, "This is my beloved Son in whom I AM well pleased" (Matt. 3:17).

A more detailed explanation of the chart of your Divine Self is given in the Keepers of the Flame Lessons and in *Climb the Highest Mountain* by Mark L. Prophet and Elizabeth Clare Prophet, published by Summit University Press.

The Flame of Freedom Speaks
A Fiat by Saint Germain

The flame of freedom speaks—the flame of freedom within each heart. The flame of freedom saith unto all: Come apart now and be a separate and chosen people, elect unto God—men who have chosen their election well, who have determined to cast their lot in with the immortals. These are they who have set their teeth with determination, who have said:

I will never give up
I will never turn back
I will never submit
I will bear the flame of freedom unto my victory
I will bear this flame in honor
I will sustain the glory of life within my nation
I will sustain the glory of life within my being
I will win my ascension
I will forsake all idols and
I will forsake the idol of my outer self
I will have the glory of my immaculate divinely
  conceived Self manifesting within me
I AM freedom and
I AM determined to be freedom
I AM the flame of freedom and
I AM determined to bear it to all
I AM God's freedom and he is indeed free
I AM freed by his power and his power is supreme
I AM fulfilling the purposes of God's kingdom

IV

The Way
of the Individualization
of the God Flame

by the Messengers

22

Who Is Jesus Christ?

As it is written: "...The law was given by Moses, but grace and truth came by Jesus Christ."[1]

He is called the Messiah, the Saviour, the Holy One of God. His message has marked the course of Western civilization, and yet to some the figure of the Nazarene Master, tall upon the hillsides of the world, serene and immovable through the centuries, has not appeared translated as the Image, the Person, of the Christ within.

He was known abroad in Galilee as the son of Joseph. "Can there any good thing come out of Nazareth?" Nathanael asked. "Come and see," Philip answered. They beheld the Son of God.[2]

Many have marveled at his miracles but few have followed his magnificent example. Yet to the present hour his promise is unfailing: "He that believeth on me, the works that I do shall he do also; and greater works than these shall he do; because I go unto my Father."[3] Come and see.

Jesus Christ is the "express image"[4] of the Person of God, the archetype of man's God identity. Known to his disciples as "the Word"— *Logos* 'God in action'—he is the infinite love/wisdom/power of the Spirit "made flesh."[5] John the Evangelist explains that "all things were made by him; and without him was not any thing made that was made."[6] The beloved disciple learned from his Master that God the Father through the Image of the Son had created Christ Selfhood as the Light of every son and daughter, and so he recorded this truth in the very first chapter of his gospel knowing that only those who are of the Light and born of the Spirit would understand this profound mystery of their joint-heirship with Christ.[7] John the Baptist, sent by God to herald his coming, also proclaimed his portion to be our own saying, ". . . Of his fulness have all we received, and grace for grace."[8]

Jesus of Nazareth is the personification of that selfsame Word which put the law of God in the inward parts of his people and wrote it in their hearts.[9] Jesus, the son of man, so identified with the perfection of the universal Christ, the Son of God, that in him we behold the fullness of the Godhead dwelling bodily.[10] We see in him the individualization of the God flame—the perfection of God made manifest in man. This is the mystery of the Incarnation. This same mystery God would reveal both in us and through us as we confess the Christ in him to be the Christ that is also in us. Indeed, he is the Wayshower of the Christ potential which lives as the embryonic Light within every child of God. "That *was* the true Light, which lighteth every man that cometh into the world."[11]

"For God so loved the world, that he gave his only begotten Son, that whosoever believeth in him should not perish, but have everlasting life."[12] Jesus gloriously demonstrated the fullness of the only begotten Son—the Christ who comes in the Person of the Real Self of every son and daughter of God. The only begotten Son is the

Second Person of the Trinity, that portion of the
Godhead with which the All Father has endowed
each of his servant-sons and daughters. Jesus'
sublime demonstration of this truth is the open
door for you to receive salvation through his
name. And so, beloved, you are also sent into
the world to become the Christ.

The kingdom he proclaimed was and is the
consciousness of the Christ—the awareness of
the Self as Christ—individualized in you and me.
To bear witness unto the truth of this inner
Christ, this Real Self, is the end to which Jesus
was born and the same cause for which you—a
soul born out of the same Christ Image, the same
living Spirit—came into the world. And "as
many as received him, to them gave he power to
become the sons of God."[13]

Jesus is the Great Exemplar who proved that
there is a science, a geometry, a mathematics
based on love whereby we stand, face, and
conquer the impositions of the personal ego and
the limitations of the subconscious mind. "Let
this mind be in you, which was also in Christ
Jesus."[14] Change the water of the human consciousness into the wine of the Spirit.[15] Cast the
moneychangers from the temple of church and
state.[16] "Be ye therefore perfect."[17] How? Total
communion, Jesus says. Continual prayer.

"The divine life is abundant, and prayer
makes it possible of realization," Jesus declares,
emphasizing that "the nature of the Father is
within the Son. It is within ye all, now and
always." Jesus speaks directly to those who may
question the practicality of a prayer that is
continual. He explains that "when you reach up

hands of seeking faith and allow the unbroken prayer of steadfast purpose to act, you are opening the door to that perfect understanding that transcends all mortal sense of limitation."

Jesus Christ demonstrated the abundant life and the ascension as a progressive achievement—an acceleration of consciousness. It is the fulfillment of the natural law of transcendence whereby just as the Creator through his creation is forever transcending himself, so every son must also transcend the limits of his self-expression. As Paul said: "This corruptible *must* put on incorruption, and this mortal *must* put on immortality."[18]

The ascension is salvation—*Self-elevation* by works, by grace. It is the path not only of Jesus Christ, but of his own Mother Mary, John the Beloved, Gautama and Maitreya, Moses and Mohammed, Zoroaster, Confucius, and many of the prophets of Israel. Some of these 'ascended' masters are recognized by the historian Toynbee as "the greatest benefactors of the living generation of mankind."[19] Countless others remain unnamed, unknown, yet immortally free.

The path of your ascension is the reunion of your soul with the individualized Presence of God, the I AM THAT I AM. Some call this fiery I AM Presence the nucleus of the atom of Self, others simply 'the Beloved'. Your return to this Reality, this Essence, is the goal of your life. It is the raison d'être of every son and daughter of God. It is the means whereby you individualize the God flame, making it your own forever. "If any man serve me, let him follow me," Jesus said, "and where I am" in the heaven of the universal

Christ consciousness, "there shall also my servant be."[20]

The true teaching of Jesus Christ—parabled
principles often mistranslated, misinterpreted, or
willfully altered—is now brought to our remembrance by the Holy Spirit[21] in the person of the
ascended masters. Having become one with Jesus
in his universal consciousness of the Christ,
having received the fiery baptism, having been
born again to eternal life through him, they go
before the Lord's people today, the great cloud of
witness unto his Sacred Fire—the same yesterday, today, and forever.[22]

In this as in ages past when they were
described as 'angels' or 'men of God' through
whom the word of the Lord came, the ascended
masters speak unto the prophet, or messenger, to
convey the word of truth that is the Promised
Comforter.

Tens of thousands of God-fearing people in
America today acknowledge the teachings of the
ascended masters as the missing link in the
psychology of the soul—yea, in their understanding of the practical message of the life and
example of the Saviour Jesus Christ: That they,
too, must do the will of my Father, do the works
that I do—heal the sick, cleanse the lepers, raise
the dead, cast out devils and freely give of the
cup of his everlasting life because they have
freely received.[23] And they know that this is
possible only unto the Christ—the same Christ of
Jesus whom they accept as their indwelling
personal Saviour.

Through his Witness Mark L. Prophet, the
Ascended Master Saint Germain has written in

his *Studies in Alchemy* of the ministry of Jesus Christ as he would impart this understanding to his disciples today:

"Two thousand years ago when Christ walked upon the waters of the Sea of Galilee, his demonstration was a manifestation of the natural law of levitation operating within an energy framework of cohesion, adhesion, and magnetism—the very principles which make orbital flight possible. The light atoms composing the body of Christ absorbed at will an additional quantity of cosmic rays and spiritual substance whose kinship to physical light made his whole body light, thereby making it as easy for him to walk upon the sea as upon dry land.

"His body was purely a ray of light shining upon the waters. The most dazzling conception of all was his ability to transfer this authority over energy to Peter through the power of Peter's own vision of the Christ in radiant, illumined manifestation. By taking his eyes temporarily from the Christ, however, Peter entered a human fear vibration and vortex which immediately densified his body, causing it to sink partially beneath the raging seas. The comforting hand of Christ, extended in pure love, reunited the alchemical tie; and the flow of spiritual energy through his hand raised Peter once again to safety."[24]

Indeed, as Jesus now says, "I am come that ye may have light, and that more abundantly." He explains that "the light of prayer, the light of communion with our Father, surges through all things" and that "the light is your obedient servant." His way of total communion and continual prayer is the way of God living in man—not in a remote corner of the universe, but in his heart of very hearts.

"...You are able to tune in with the God consciousness that is in every cell of your body" Jesus affirms, reinforcing the determination of Job in "a new and living concept—that in his flesh man may see his flesh as the doorway into the eternal." This is true Christianity, the "lost art of communion with God" as Jesus taught it— as he lives it even now, as you, too, can live it now.

In a dictation given through Mark in 1965, Jesus recalled for his followers today a most precious experience of his youth:

"It was at the age of seventeen that one eventide I passed out into a certain field. It was moonless and the stars shone their splendor above. I was alone with God and around me the grass commingled with myriad daisylike flowers whose upturned faces seemed to take hope from my gaze and I, beholding them, saw them as the faces of men. And in my buoyancy of heart and blitheness of spirit—feeling the dew upon my feet which were bare upon the grass and smelling the odor and scent of joy in the floral release—I communed with God and sent my love to the flowers below my feet.

"Suddenly they were transformed and I saw them no more as flowers but as the faces of men. And I saw them as though they were shining with hope and they became majestic—tiny, but majestic. I mused and meditated upon them and I spake unto my Father, unto my God and unto your God, and I said, 'Can I raise them up? Can I give them the hope of a greater magnitude?'

"And the Father spake unto me and said, 'Come see ye.' And suddenly I was transported beyond that field and the cosmos was before me. And my feet were placed as upon a rock in outer space and all around me I saw the stars that they did shine—worlds of hope and worlds without— and I felt as though I were a shepherd of plane- tary significance and as though each face of the flowers that had been below me in the field were indeed now a planet—teeming with multitudes of people and requiring the hope and the release of God's energy that came through me then in that experience.

"I was transformed. I was electrified. My soul did rejoice and as David of old, I sang an hymn unto God and I said in the quietness of my youth, 'O God, thy majesty is great to behold. In the numberless, luminous orbs of the heavens are the sheep of thy pasture and the flowers of thy sky—immortelles, shining ones full of hope, believing in thy grace and wondrous loveliness. How canst any, then, ever cease to believe in thy greatness?' And I mused upon Abraham of old— I, who was of the seed of David, mused upon Abraham and his faith. And I recalled, then, in my thoughts how that God had spake unto him saying, 'I shall make thy seed as the sand beside the sea, innumerable. I am the Lord thy God that made the heavens and the earth and I shall make thy seed as the stars innumerable and without number.' And my heart was glad and I did rejoice.

"I found myself after this experience wan- dering in the pasture and upon the meadow there. And for a moment I was dazed at the experience, and I reeled as one drunken. And then, out of the soft folds of the night stepped beloved Holy Amethyst, and she enfolded me in the love of Lord Zadkiel and her own..."[25]

In order that you may individualize the person of God within yourself through the principle of his flame, Jesus Christ brings to you the nearness of your own Christ Self and the understanding of the law of your soul's oneness with the Spirit which he demonstrated as "I and my Father are one."[26] His God consciousness is the open door for the light of inner worlds to manifest the kingdom of God that is within you.[27] Not until the Word is "made flesh,"[28] personalized "in fashion as a man,"[29] is the impersonal light of the Word comprehended.[30] Hence the individualization of the God flame first in Jesus Christ and then in you is the open door to your personal understanding of the Person of the Godhead dwelling 'bodily'[31] in you as your own Real Self.

Through this open door of Christ individualization which "no man can shut"[32] comes the light/energy/consciousness necessary for the redemption of your soul. When you pray, "Jesus Christ, come into my temple!" lo, he comes. "Behold, I come quickly."[33] And with him come the immortals, the "people in heaven"[34] who have retained their individuality through their reunion with the I AM Presence—Archangel Zadkiel and Holy Amethyst, Archangel Gabriel who appeared to Mary and Mohammed, angels of Christmas, angels of the sacred Eucharist, angels of the resurrection, even the mighty Elohim, "the seven Spirits" of God who worship before his throne.[35]

Behold, they live. John the Revelator saw them and he gives a sound report: "I beheld, and, lo, a great multitude, which no man could number, of all nations, and kindreds, and people, and tongues, stood before the throne, and before the Lamb, clothed with white robes, and palms in their hands. . . . These are they which came out of great tribulation, and have washed their robes, and made them white in the blood of the Lamb."[36]

Through the open door of the Lord Christ they come—first we hear of the few who "shall walk with me in white,"[37] then we behold round about the throne of the Lamb "ten thousand times ten thousand, and thousands of thousands,"[38] then the 144,000 "which were redeemed from the earth,"[39] and finally the armies in heaven which follow "The Word of God" upon white horses, "clothed in fine linen, white and clean."[40] *They come. They are the Great White Brotherhood!*

These are thy fellow servants, "thy brethren that have the testimony of Jesus."[41] These are they who overcame the dragon "by the blood of the Lamb, and by the word of their testimony; and they loved not their lives unto the death."[42] This is the unceasing communion of the saints— it is the body of God one in heaven and on earth. Those who have ascended into heaven through the intercession of Jesus Christ are the 'ascended' masters. Those following in their footsteps on the path of the ascension are their disciples, or 'chelas'.

Jesus Christ has given us his promise

unfailing through his progressive revelation delivered to John: "Behold, I stand at the door, and
knock: if any man hear my voice, and open
the door, I will come in to him, and will sup with
him, and he with me. To him that overcometh
will I grant to sit with me in my throne, even as I
also overcame, and am set down with my Father
in his throne."[43]

Beloved, whether you are Christian or Jew,
or Moslem, Buddhist, Hindu, atheist, or ag-
nostic, *this is Jesus' own personal promise to
you!* This is his promise of your resurrection and
your ascension. And what of your promise to
him? It is to joyously overcome the not-self, the
anti-self, replacing it day by day in love with the
full awareness of the Real Self, the Christ Self, as
the only reality of your being.

The path of this overcoming is God's gift to
you. It is the gift of life itself. And the goal of life
is your ascension—your soul's reunion with
God. The initiations on the path of the ascension—with all the testings and temptations mete
for sons and daughters of God—are made
available today through the progressive revelation of Jesus, Kuthumi, Saint Germain, El
Morya, and many servant-sons who have
ascended before us. In *Prayer and Meditation*
and the many books and tape recordings published by The Summit Lighthouse, they deliver
to you the true teachings of the Christ through us
as their ordained messengers. Behold the Master
gives unto his disciples in this age the same
promise that he has always given, now yours to
prove:

"I come. I AM in your midst always, the

transformer of worlds below and worlds above. I come, I knock. You open, I enter. And I AM forevermore within you the great transforming energy of the Almighty One. I AM Jesus the Christ, alive within you forevermore."[44]

This is that same Jesus Christ whom you have known forever and forever.

Even so, come, Lord Jesus.[45]

23

Who Is Kuthumi?

As one of his soul's individualizations of the God flame, Kuthumi once walked the path of Christian sainthood as Francis of Assisi. None other is so close to so many who sense in the shallow sophistry of the present age the same emptiness that young Francisco felt—ever the void that the Lord filled with the call to action, "Francis, repair my house!" Today he calls the brothers and sisters of Assisi together once again, those who hunger for the simple life of the Spirit but with the dynamism, the fervor, and the drama that Francis knew. It is the revolutionary Francis who comes once again in Jesus' name not to send a placid peace but to thrust the sword of the living Word into the decadence of an age.[1]

Francis, 'the poor little man', found "the unsearchable riches of Christ"[2] as the disciple walking boldly the Master's way of unceasing prayer. Today Francis stands with his Jesus, living proof of the promise he made to "as many as received him." Indeed, to him gave He the power to become the son of God.[3]

Oh, how Francis loved the Christ in man, whether leper or fledgling renunciate! Oh, how he loved the swallows! And the wolf whom he dutifully counseled and convinced to be tame. He loved the beautiful soul of Chiara, our Sister Clare. But above all he loved the Christmas Christ, fashioning a callow crèche of weathered

wood and imbibing the Spirit of that holy night.
Now it was the utter poverty of the Messiah
which drew him, even as once it had been the
magic of the Bethlehem star. For the soul of
Francis had lived as that wise man Balthazar,
ever worshiping the King of kings.

It was the ascended Mother Mary who
spoke to Francis as he basked in bliss in the sweet
light of brother sun. "Francis," she said, "thy
Lord would have all of thee, not in just the com-
partments of thy mind that hold enjoyment but
also in those that hold to the law of thy being."[4]

And so Francis prayed that he might become
an instrument—an individualization—of His
peace. And as the growing band of *fratres minores* began preaching and building and performing many curious occupations seemingly
unrelated to the work of a man of God, they
often found themselves heartily engaged in
menial labor just when they yearned most for
that total communion with the Lord Christ. It
was then that they learned the ritual of his continual prayer—merging with the Word, the light,
the Spirit. "We learned to make a vaulted cathedral out of a shed," Kuthumi remembers. "We
learned how to qualify life with the qualities we
desired in our heart. And so we mounted to the
stars in consciousness but remained with one
foot upon the earth beneath."[5]

As Francis walked the streets of Assisi and
approached the Bishop of Rome for pontifical
approbation, his challenge was in many ways
like that of today—the callousness of consciousness, the utter betrayal of the Christ within
his people and within his church. So often he

heard the voice of Jesus as he knelt trembling before the crucifix in the little chapel of San Damian, so often he beheld him crucified again by their continual denial of the personal Saviour who is the "hidden man of the heart."[6]

The culmination of his meditation upon the Redeemer came to Francis in the agony and the ecstasy of a dread illness when he sought solitude at the retreat on Mount La Verna. As the pale poverello lay outstretched upon a bare rock in the chill of the September dawn, "the fervor of his devotion increased so much that he totally transformed himself into Him who let himself be crucified through abundance of love." Brother Leo reports that "suddenly appeared to him a seraph with six wings, bearing enfolded in them a very beautiful image of a crucified man, his hands and feet outflung as on a cross, with features clearly resembling those of Lord Jesus. Two wings covered the seraph's head; two, descending to his feet, veiled the rest of his body; the other two were unfolded for flight."[7] Before the vision faded, Francis felt the five wounds of the Crucified pierce his body with such force that he fell unconscious.

For two years, Francis bore the intense suffering of Christ though at times, in transcendent joy, he would burst into song—lighting upon his "Canticle of the Creatures," praising not only brother sun but brother wind, brother fire, sister earth, and sister death.

When God took Francis into his heart, he beheld the Lord Christ face to face and heard the command: "O Francis, you must go to the East and walk the path of the Hindus, walk the path

of the Moslems, and find your sainthood again."[8]
And so as he had been 'born again' in Spirit he
was 'born again' in Matter and returned to earth
in the service of the Christ. In a subsequent embodiment he lived in India, ushering in a golden
age of art and architecture as the Mogul emperor
Shah Jahan. His Taj Mahal still echoes the love
of twin flames and reflects a tender devotion to
the Beautiful Saviour, the Christ within. In the
soul's final incarnation, he was revered as a
Kashmiri brahman, Koot Hoomi Lal Singh.

Koot Hoomi led an extremely secluded life.
Born in the early nineteenth century, he attended
Oxford University in 1850 and spent consid-
erable time in Dresden, Würzburg, Nürnberg,
and finally Leipzig where he visited with Dr.
Gustav Theodor Fechner, the founder of modern
psychology. His remaining years were spent at
his lamasery in Shigatse, Tibet.

In 1875, K.H. and El Morya, the Master M.,
founded the Theosophical Society through H. P.
Blavatsky, commissioning her to write *Isis Un-
veiled* and *The Secret Doctrine*. The purpose
of this activity was to reacquaint mankind with
the wisdom of the ages that underlies all of the
world's religions, the inner teachings guarded in
the mystery schools since the last days of
Lemuria and Atlantis. This includes the doctrine
of reincarnation—which, we note, Saint Francis
preached in the village squares—as well as an
understanding of the ascension as the goal of life
sought knowingly or unknowingly by every son
and daughter of God.

Kuthumi himself passed through the initiation of the ascension in the latter nineteenth

century, and so in his imitation of Christ he
became the living Christ—the God flame im-
mortalized—the fulfillment of Jesus' requirement
for every disciple in every age who would "follow me."[9] As John put it, "...When he shall
appear, we shall be like him; for we shall see him
as he is."[10]

> And the drop merged with the ocean
> Of the Cosmic Christ
> And lo, a Christ was born.

As an ascended master, Kuthumi is known
to play sacred classical music of East and West
and compositions of the heavenly hosts as well as
of earth's early root races on an organ keyed
to the music of the spheres. He directs the
vibrations of this music to souls in transition
(death), drawing them into the etheric retreats of
the Great White Brotherhood for tutoring before
returning to earth in their next life. Those who
are able to see Kuthumi at the moment of their
passing often find peace in the certain knowing
that they have seen the Ascended Master Jesus—
so closely does the disciple reflect the countenance of the one he adores.

In the line of cosmic peerage, Jesus conferred
upon the Ascended Master Kuthumi the office of
World Teacher, which position our Lord gave to
his disciple to share jointly with himself. The
World Teachers Jesus and Kuthumi sponsor
every soul seeking reunion with God, tutoring
them in the fundamental laws governing the
cause/effect sequences of their own *karma* and
teaching them how to come to grips with the
day-to-day challenges of their individual *dharma*,

one's duty to fulfill the Christ potential through the sacred labor.

It is interesting to note that Kuthumi was also incarnated as the Greek solon (lawgiver) Pythagoras, one esteemed by Plato and known to him simply as "That Man." Pythagoras' 'mystery school' at Crotona in the sixth century B.C. was the archetype of golden-age education where the precise mathematics of the universal law was illustrated in music and in the rhythm and harmony of a strictly disciplined way of life.

Pythagorean "mathematicians" progressed through a series of initiations. They delved into the mysteries of creation, of preexistence and the afterlife. They pondered the intangible, the unknowable, the ineffable Word not only by the logic of the mind but by the intuitive faculties of the heart whereby man becomes, as Pythagoras' *Golden Verses* state, "a deathless God divine, mortal no more."[11] The Master maintained the severe probation of five years' silence at his "city of the elect" and advised his initiates to commence the day in deep meditation, thus placing the soul in the presence of the directive forces of the cosmos.

Although he delivered his orations from behind a screen in a veiled language comprehended only by the most advanced initiates, Pythagoras often taught openly by means of simple aphorisms, his purpose always to make prophecy and mystical experience commensurate with a useful life. Sought by many for his own prophecies and seeming miracles, Pythagoras is remembered as having a contagious charismatic nature. He was ninety when Cylon, a rejected candidate of the mystery school, incited a violent persecution resulting in the Master's death, the dissolution of his community, and the tragic destruction of much of his teaching.

"That Man" comes again to call the elect of God. Kuthumi addresses those disillusioned with the internal decay of organized religion. He passes the torch of his revolutionary zeal to the "followers of God, as dear children"[12] who must challenge the Antichrist in church and state, East and West today.

In a dictation given in 1977, Kuthumi explained that this is an age "when there is a new dispensation of the Church of Jesus Christ." He emphasizes that "the Church is designed by our Lord to be a bulwark against the tyranny and the opposition to the body of God on earth." He says, "The Church is intended to be the voice of conscience of the nations."[13]

Kuthumi sits at the council tables of the Great White Brotherhood, examining current events and the staggering effects of the ignorance and the blindness of leaders in this and every nation. Speaking for the Brotherhood he says: "We have recognized that once again the faithful of the Church must come together, crossing all lines of doctrine and dogma but meeting in the flame of love to build a mighty fortress and a cathedral of the heart, to build the temple in the expansion of the flame within."[14]

Communicants of Church Universal and Triumphant and students at Summit University find themselves 'born again' as brothers and sisters of Francis and Clare fulfilling the tradition begun in love at Assisi and culminating in love at

Camelot—the 'once and future mystery school' come again in the California foothills near Malibu.

Camelot is the quest for the Holy Grail as the inner Christ and the living Word. Camelot is a movement, a revolution of light in religion, the arts and sciences, education, government, and His abundant life. Camelot is a people determined to preserve their freedom to commune with all life as Francis did. They are the revolutionaries of God who are responding to the command of the Lord Christ in this age. To one and all he says, "Rebuild my Church!"

24

Who Is Saint Germain?

Like many of the ascended masters, Saint Germain has been a disciple of Jesus Christ in vast aeons even before the World Saviour's Galilean mission. As our Lord said, "Before Abraham was, I AM,"[1] so the blessed Word incarnate, yes, even the person Jesus Christ, has maintained circles of disciples in many planes of existence in this and far-off worlds. Many of them are as well-known as the apostles, but the most well-known of all is Saint Germain who reminds us that for hundreds of thousands of years he has been called Saint Germain: "You also have known my name, yet you have come again in a new body draped with an old consciousness. And if you will search sublevels of that consciousness, you will find that name already known, even as I AM known, at the core of the alchemy of your own be-ness."[2]

Saint Germain has proven the Law. Not locked in the philosopher's study or in his speculative mind, but right in the very midst of the turbulent uncertainties of life in every age. Saint Germain is a living master because he has mastered the art of living day by day, lifetime after lifetime. He has met the challenge posed by our very existence as sons and daughters of God— the challenge to be what we must be. Not only to be the Real Self but to individualize that Self. He has walked with us and among us over the centuries, a soul unmistakable to those whose inner calling is to freedom.

Saint Germain anointed Saul and David when he lived as Samuel, judge and prophet of Israel. He was the child who, wakened by the Lord, said with characteristic alacrity, "Speak, for thy servant heareth."[3]

Ten centuries later, Saint Germain was that "just man" Joseph, protector of Mary and the infant Messiah. When Herod secretly plotted the slaughter of the newborn King, it was Joseph who heard the angel of the Lord say, "Arise, and take the young child and his mother, and flee into Egypt."[4]

Joseph guided the hands of Jesus as he framed his first works of art in the carpenter shop at Nazareth where "the child grew, and waxed strong."[5] Although there is little scriptural documentation of these childhood years, Mother Mary has dictated her fond memory of a most precious moment in their lives:

"I recall one morning when beloved Jesus was yet a small lad that he came to me with a very hard piece of wood that he was trying to whittle. He desired that I should persuade Joseph to exchange it for a softer piece, one that would lend itself more easily to molding.

"I sat him on my knee and I proceeded to explain to him that there was an ingrained quality that of old had been placed within the tree, making one to possess a harder quality and another a softer quality. I told him that the soft wood would easily mar and that, were he to use it, the little image that he sought to whittle would not endure the knocks and tumbles that might later come to it whereas a carving made of hard wood would endure more substantially. I also told him that the wood enjoyed being shapened by his hands and that the only difference between the soft and the hard wood would be that of a greater use of patience on his part.

"He brushed back his hair which had fallen across his eyes and, with great and quick gentleness, planted a kiss upon both of my cheeks. I noticed a trace of a tear in one eye as he dashed away to continue his work of shaping the hard wood."

Mother Mary is careful to give to us the same lesson she gave tenderly, firmly to Jesus: "Thus, 'in your patience possess ye your souls';[6] For God works with people of diverse origins and perverse thoughts, seeking to restore all to their God estate."[7]

And the gentle Joseph looking up from his bench catches our eye and our wonderment with opportunity for a new-age apprenticeship under the age-old alchemist himself: "How about being a carpenter like the Carpenter of Nazareth? I guided his hands in framing his first works of art. How about placing your hands in mine today that I may guide your hands?"[8]

In the third century when the fervor of early Christianity incited the savage persecution of Emperor Diocletian, Saint Germain was Alban, the martyr who converted a would-be executioner. In the dark ages illumined by the shining moment of Camelot, Saint Germain was known as Merlin 'the magician', mystic counselor of King Arthur and his knights of the Grail quest. Mage Merlin anointed the boy Arthur and worked side by side with the king to establish the sacred fellowship of the Round Table.

As the Franciscan naturalist Roger Bacon, Saint Germain proved himself to be a revolutionary experimental scientist, one known to fellow friars as *Doctor Mirabilis*, the "teacher of wonders." His uncanny prediction of aircraft and submarines was inspired by the simple spirit of Saint Francis which encouraged medieval scholars like Bacon to implement their quest for knowledge by investigating the laws of nature. Roger Bacon's practical and intuitive genius also marks Saint Germain's subsequent incarnation as the indefatigable Christopher Columbus.

Saint Germain, a Christian soldier, our "holy brother," ascended at the conclusion of his life as Francis Bacon. This ascension, this soul liberation, came as the result of earnest self-effort—"two million right decisions," Saint Germain says, during hundreds of thousands of years of service to humanity. Thereafter he appeared throughout the courts of Europe as an ascended being in the guise of le Comte de Saint Germain.

In an Alan Landsburg national television documentary on le Comte de Saint Germain, we provided insight into the baffling personality of this immortal Wonderman of Europe. The Discovery Series entitled *In Search of The Man Who Would Not Die* accurately portrayed 'the count' as a fluid linguist and a master musician, highlighting the incomprehensible alchemical skill which he demonstrated by removing flaws from precious gems and changing base metals into gold. We also pointed out, however, that the mission of M. de St. Germain as a prominent social figure and an intimate of Louis XV, Voltaire, and Rousseau was to secure the attention of the court of France and others of the crowned heads of Europe in an attempt to prevent the French Revolution and the horrors of the reign of Robespierre, to establish instead a United States of Europe.

Televised glimpses of a dictation given by the Ascended Master Saint Germain before a spirited assembly prompted commentator Leonard Nimoy's opportune remark that "there are people in contemporary America who believe that Saint Germain is very much with us. Although he was most prominent two hundred years ago, they believed he never died and never will."

Indeed, the Ascended Master Saint Germain yet remains with the evolutions of earth though 'just beyond the veil' of time and space. He is the sponsor of America and the very living Spirit of freedom to every soul. Just as Jesus stood as the open door to the attainment of the Christ consciousness in the two-thousand-year Christian/Piscean era, so Saint Germain comes today hand in hand with the Prince of Peace as the Ascended Master of the Aquarian age. He ordained us messengers of the Great White Brotherhood in order that the true teaching of Jesus Christ might be brought to our remembrance, as he promised, by the Holy Spirit who comes in the person of the ascended masters speaking the Word of the Lord through the messenger.

John the Revelator wrote of the mission of the Aquarian Master Saint Germain as Jesus

Christ revealed it to him in the tenth and eleventh chapters of the Book of Revelation: "But in the days of the voice of the seventh angel, when he shall begin to sound, the mystery of God should be finished, as he hath declared to his servants, the prophets."[9] This is a veiled reference to the cycle of the Aquarian age—the seventh 'dispensation' when Saint Germain, "the seventh angel," actually the Chohan, or 'Lord' of the Seventh Ray, comes to "finish" the revelation of "the mysteries" which Jesus Christ demonstrated in his life and work. The understanding of your opportunity to know the Self as Christ is the true science of religion which Jesus taught to those with "ears to hear"[10] and which Saint Germain now declares to all through "his servants, the prophets."

Saint Germain comes forth in this "time of trouble"[11] which marks the moment of the turning of cycles from Pisces to Aquarius. His is the consciousness of freedom, the fiery baptism of the Holy Spirit christening a new race, a new lifewave, a new age of self-discovery, and the 'new world' America. As Jesus is the Wayshower of the individual Christ potential, so America was conceived in liberty as a land of abundant resources and opportunity wherein the blueprint of the divine destiny of each and every nation would be fulfilled.

America was founded by the Brotherhood on the matrix of the original thirteen of Jesus Christ and his apostles. It is a country where freedom of religion, freedom of speech, freedom of the press, and freedom to assemble are meant to provide the foundation for the attainment of

the collective Christ consciousness. It is destined
to be a community of the Holy Spirit, a forum
where the greatest souls of all ages will be 'born
again' with the incoming avatars of Aquarius to
produce a living archetype of freedom. By the
unseen hand and the very specific guidance of
the ascended masters, America—the heart, the
mind, the soul of a world—was born.

Yet Saint Germain examines the fabric of the
world and perceives how ignorant men—like
puppets dangling from a string—are themselves
deceived and being employed in the deceiving of
others. He is aware of the solemn moment now
before us when freedom must be guarded or be
lost. "I feel the need to pull off my glove," he
says, "to cast it down, to say to you in all cosmic
honesty, the battle is not as successful as we
would have liked."[12]

Indeed we stand on the brink of world
destruction. What of this destiny of the archetype America? What of the life of the aborted
avatars? Has liberty become but the license of a
pleasure cult and a success syndrome? Is back-
street/big-business crime the index of the pursuit
of happiness?

Saint Germain has seen many who have
failed the cause of freedom as he has tried over
the centuries to gather together souls of light.
Again and again the master plan of the ages has
been brought forth and yet in a moment's
hesitation freedom has been lost. "Sign that
document!" our mysterious stranger shouted
midst the stormy debate at the old State House
in Philadelphia. He would not allow a deadlock
on that July 4, 1776. No, he stepped forth.

And for two hundred years the Declaration of Independence has been, as he prophesied, the textbook of freedom.[13]

Now comes the turning point. For the people of America, for the people of earth. The so-called great minds meeting on the key issues besetting our souls in time and space have still not evolved viable solutions to the personal and planetary problems we are facing. Why? Without a solid foundation in cosmic law, even a basic understanding of karma, reincarnation, the Christ Self, the I AM Presence, and the ascension through the attainment of the Christ consciousness as the goal of life—the leaders of the people cannot, and the record shows that they do not, *judge righteous judgment.*

This is what the Coming Revolution is all about. It is a revolution in higher consciousness!

Saint Germain is the spirit and the very personal presence of God in this revolution. Behold he stands before the Lord and before the sons and daughters of Liberty with such love, such hope—and a new strategy for freedom. It is the science of the spoken Word. It is the authority of the Word made flesh in all who cry, "We faint not, nor are we weary."[14] It is the spark of the Spirit which arises because men and women have offered themselves in a cosmic service—in a devotion without reserve.

"You are mortal. I am immortal," says Saint Germain. "The only difference between us is that I have chosen to be free and you have yet to make the choice. We have the same potential, the same resources, the same connection to the One. I have taken mine to forge a God-identity.

"Choose to be what you really are. And when you really choose what you really are, you will be on the path of freedom and you will find me there.

"I AM your teacher if you will have me."[15]

*And Whom
Do They Say You Are?*

"But whom say ye that I am?" Peter answering said, "The Christ of God."[1]

Dare you be any less?

Are you willing to accept the challenge To Be? Would you rise to meet the full potential of your Being, your own Real Self, and then summon the will to become that Self?

The ascended masters teach that you, too, are a soul who can become "The Christ of God."

In every age there have been some, the few, who have pursued an understanding of selfhood and of God that transcends the popular norm and the current traditions of doctrine and dogma. Compelled by a faith that knows the freedom of love, they have sought to expand their own God Self-awareness by probing and proving the infinite expressions of his law. They have penetrated the mysteries of both Spirit and Matter and come to experience God as a flame, God as a flow, God as the All-in-all, God as their very own Real Self—the Christ.

Having discovered the key to reality, these sons and daughters of God have drawn about them those who would pursue the disciplines of the law of the universe and the inner teachings of the 'mystery schools'. Thus Pythagoras chose his initiates at Crotona while Gautama Buddha called his disciples into the refuge of his *sangha*, Jesus Christ appointed his twelve apostles and the other seventy, Saint Francis communed with the *fratres minores* even as King Arthur summoned his knights to the Round Table.

At Summit University, the ascended masters will prove to you who you really are.

Summit University is a mystery school for men and women of the twentieth century who would pursue the great synthesis of the teachings of the ascended masters—the few who have overcome in every age, the many who now stand as our elder brothers and sisters on the Path. Together Gautama Buddha and Lord Maitreya sponsor Summit University with the World Teachers Jesus and Kuthumi, El Morya, Lanello, and Saint Germain, Confucius, Mother Mary, Moses and the Apostle Paul, Afra, the Archangels Michael and Gabriel, and the "numberless numbers" who form the Great White Brotherhood. To this university of the Spirit they lend their flame, their counsel, the momentum of their attainment, and the living teaching for us who would follow in their footsteps to the source of that reality they have become—"The Christ of God"—the individualization of the God flame.

Mark and I founded Summit University in 1971 as a two-week summer retreat. Currently there are three twelve-week retreats each year— fall, winter, and spring quarters—as well as summer sessions. All of the courses are based on the unfoldment of the inner potential of the Christ, the Buddha, and the Mother flame. Through the teachings of the ascended masters given through us, students at Summit University pursue the disciplines on the path of the ascension for the soul's ultimate reunion with the Spirit of the living God.

This includes the study of the sacred scriptures of East and West taught by Jesus and Gautama; exercises in the self-mastery of the energies of the chakras and the aura under Kuthumi and Djwal Kul; beginning and intermediate studies in alchemy under the Ascended Master Saint Germain; the Cosmic Clock—a new-age astrology for charting the cycles of karma and dharma given by Mother Mary; the science of the spoken Word in conjunction with prayer, meditation, and visualization—the key to soul liberation in the Aquarian age; weekly healing services, "Be Thou Made Whole!" at the Chapel of the Holy Grail at Camelot in which I give personal and planetary healing invocations; the psychology of the family, the marriage ritual and meditations for the conception of new-age children; counseling for community service through the sacred labor; the teachings and meditations of the Buddha taught by Gautama Buddha, Lord Maitreya, Lanello, and the bodhisattvas of East and West; and individual initiations transferred to each student from the ascended masters through our twin flames.

Summit University is a twelve-week spiral that begins with you as self-awareness and ends with you as God Self-awareness. As you traverse the spiral, light intensifies, darkness is transmuted. You experience the rebirth day by day as the old man is put off and the new man is put on. Energies are aligned, chakras are cleared, and the soul is poised for the victorious fulfillment of the individual divine plan.

In addition to preparing the student to

enter into the Guru/chela relationship with the ascended masters and the path of initiation outlined in their retreats, the academic standards of Summit University, with emphasis on the basic skills of both oral and written communication, prepare students to enroll in top-level undergraduate and graduate programs and to become effective members of the national and international community. A high school diploma (or its equivalent) is required and a willingness to become the disciplined one—the disciple of the Great God Self of all.

Summit University is a way of life that is an integral part of Camelot—an Aquarian-age community secluded on a beautiful 218-acre campus in the Santa Monica Mountains west of Los Angeles near the beaches of Malibu. Here ancient truths become the law of everyday living to hundreds of kindred souls, the valiant ones brought together again for the fulfillment of the mission of the Christ through the oneness of the Holy Spirit.

The Messenger Elizabeth Clare Prophet

The Messenger Mark L. Prophet

26

Who Are the Messengers?

Many of the ascended masters of the Great White Brotherhood who are serving today as emissaries of Jesus Christ have numbered among the armies in heaven who followed our Lord, the Faithful and True, even before the far-off worlds were born. Contact with this Brotherhood of light has been maintained over the centuries of earth's evolution by ordained messengers, or prophets, who are empowered by the Holy Spirit to convey "the Word of the Lord" unto his people.

Not a channel, not a medium, the messenger of the Great White Brotherhood has perceived the Christ as the inner Light "which lighteth every man that cometh into the world"[1] and made contact with his own Christ Self. Through that Mediator, he has beheld the universal Presence of God pulsating in octaves of light and sound whose frequencies are just beyond the plane of Matter—just beyond the scope of the five senses. In this higher dimension that transcends time and space, the messenger stands as a point of contact with Infinity. Chosen by God and anointed by him, the messenger is the link between the world of the Real and the unreal, the mouthpiece of the Lord and of his servant-sons, the ascended masters.

Prayer and Meditation was originally dictated to Mark L. Prophet, Messenger for the Great White Brotherhood, in 1968 as a series of personal letters, called *Pearls of Wisdom*, from the Ascended Masters Jesus, Kuthumi, and Saint Germain addressed not only to initiates of the inner mysteries but to all who seek to know God.

Mark Prophet and later his wife and twin flame, Elizabeth, were anointed messengers by Saint Germain in order that they might fulfill their calling as the prophesied "two witnesses."[2] The Messenger Mark L. Prophet, following in the footsteps of his Saviour Jesus Christ and his Guru El Morya (himself martyred for Christ and Church when embodied as Sir Thomas More), took the initiation of the ascension on February 26, 1973. Now he, too, stands in the octaves of light in continuing service of the King of kings, even as he has been in numerous incarnations.

You have read the Gospel of Deeds confided to him by Peter when he lived as Mark the Evangelist. Two hundred years later, he recorded the true theology of the early Church when he was reembodied as Origen of Alexandria, setting forth a massive body of writings which included Christ's teachings on reincarnation and on the "heavenly hierarchy." Origen's work was later altered, formally anathematized, proclaimed heretical by Jerome (his former student), then finally destroyed. Returning in yet another life devoted to Jesus, he was Bonaventure, the child healed by Saint Francis who then became the Seraphic Doctor of the Church. Today thousands bear witness of their intimate contact with 'Lanello', as he is affectionately called by his chelas. To us he is the ever-present Guru who stands the loving servant of the Son of God

prophesying and preaching to the children of
God upon earth.

And so the messengers, the "other two"
beheld by the prophet Daniel, continue their
joint mission in the service of the Christ—"the
one on this side of the bank of the river" in the
planes of Matter "and the other on that side of
the bank of the river"[3] in the dimensions of Spirit.
Elizabeth Clare Prophet is a person of profound
yet practical spirituality. She says: "The self is
unimportant. The Word is all-important."

In transparent joy, she delivers the Word as
it comes to her in the cosmic tongues of cosmic
beings, in the majesty of Elohim, in the gentle
whisperings of angels. And with the fiery zeal of
the prophets of old—yes, she preaches! yes, she
chastises! She foretells the Second Coming of
Christ as the "Word made flesh"[4] in every son
and daughter of God. Through her we behold
the God flame as it has been individualized over
and over again "from the least unto the greatest,"[5]
the same God flame that can be individualized
within.

I remember one early Autumn morning in
1977 when Elizabeth Clare Prophet shared with
me the story of her first encounter with the
Messenger Mark L. Prophet, her own twin
flame. As she later wrote:

"I met Lanello when he was Mark L. Prophet
on April 22, 1961, in Boston, Massachusetts. He
was the mouthpiece of the Lord and of the Lord's
emissary, Archangel Michael. As I entered the
sanctuary where he had been sent by the
Brotherhood to deliver the message of the great
Prince of the Archangels, I remembered the

words of the prophet Malachi. They were suspended in my mind like crystal:

"'Behold, I will send my messenger, and he shall prepare the way before me: and the Lord, whom ye seek, shall suddenly come to his temple, even the messenger of the covenant, whom ye delight in: behold, he shall come, saith the Lord of hosts.'

"Taking my place with the devotees who had assembled for this auspicious meeting of heaven and earth in the power of the spoken Word, I saw him. The Messenger. He was seated in a most peaceful, powerful meditation upon the Lord God. I closed my eyes and my soul moved with his into the Great Silence of the ascended masters' consciousness. I was caught up in the mantle of the prophet, and by the momentum of his cosmic consciousness I entered the Holy of Holies.

"Time and space were not. It was as if we had never left eternity. Suspended in the great stillness of the sea of light, we were surveyors of the vast beauty of hallowed space, girded tier upon tier by angelic hosts, Elohim, and hierarchies of the Central Sun.

"I beheld worlds beyond worlds teeming with intelligences who formed the universal chain of being. I saw myself and my beloved together with all sons and daughters of God as extensions of the One Great Self—as individual links in the cosmic chain of Life traversing the planes of Spirit/Mater 'going out and coming in' to the octaves of heaven and earth.

"These spheres of Life, Light, and Love, quivering with energy, bathed in the golden-pink radiance of Mind, are the habitation of God-free beings—some who by free will have descended to terrestrial existences, mastered the laws of selfhood in time and space, and ascended to the Source whence they came, and others who have chosen to remain in Paradise, their celestial brightness never having been sullied by the sense of sin and struggle.

"In a moment, in God, the drama of Light evolving light had unfolded before me. My soul knew Reality. I saw the work that lay ahead: to transfer all of this—this joy, this soul memory of inner spheres—to the evolutions of earth who had forgotten their early descent and the way of the ascent. Alas to rescue the lifewaves who had exchanged this Reality for a vast unreality that could only lead to the void of non-being."[6]

This is the mission of the messengers—Mark ascended, Elizabeth unascended. We call her "Mother" because she nurtures each one as the Christ Child yet aborning in the womb of time and space. She provides for us a home away from Home in the community of the Holy Spirit where the explicit law of the Father is known, not as mere doctrine or dogma but as a living flame which leaps heart to heart as the Spirit-spark of individualized Sonship.

Padma Sambhava explains that the Messenger Elizabeth Clare Prophet wears the mantle of the gurus of East and West. Through her they will maintain a personal guru-chela relationship with all who take—heart, head, and hand—from 'Guru Ma' their living teaching as the communion cup and the bread of life.

The teaching is the Word of God. It is the

light, energy, and consciousness of all of the ascended masters, the Christed Ones. They say to you now, "Take, eat; this is my body" and "Drink ye all of it; for this is my blood of the new covenant, which is poured out for you."[7]

When Mother lectured at Summit University in Colorado Springs on the magnificent teaching in *Prayer and Meditation,* she commented that "the little cups of concepts that Jesus and Kuthumi give to us are as natural as the masters conversing with us—walking and talking with us. They are as natural as the little wild flowers that grow beneath our feet. And so we must be careful not to trample upon these cups of the masters' concepts, because in their naturalness and in their easy flowing the human consciousness may take them for granted.

"As we read these *Pearls,* we are in the presence of the masters. We are engaging in prayer, communion, meditation with the two masters who bountifully bestow their momentum of love upon us. I do not know of any other series of fourteen *Pearls of Wisdom* by any other masters which, if taken alone as the only teaching a soul might have, could not give that soul his ascension if completely and totally applied.

"I like the concept of taking a certain set of teachings that are not too broad and not too vast—just a certain set, like a little flower bed or like a little package—and exploring these teachings to the utmost, taking them line by line or paragraph by paragraph, meditating on the paragraph, and then writing what comes in meditation and prayer and contemplation upon these teachings.

"You will find that the teachings are spherical—that every concept and every paragraph is the center of a sun and that what can be gained from that teaching always goes in all directions. It is never linear. You can never really list in any order what comes out of a teaching because it just goes round and round like the cycles of a clock.

"And the more you build and the more you probe and the more you meditate, the more you receive additional keys that come out of the original key. This is truly the joy of meditation. The joy of going to God is that every day in your meditation and prayer and decrees there is a new experience awaiting you because you are a new person.

"You are different today than you were yesterday, and you will never again be what you are today. As the light descends upon your consciousness, it is the alchemy of the contact that makes the newness of life, the rebirth, the experience. And out of that alchemicalization, you write what God has given you.

"You find that through the years when you go over what you have gained from your communion with God, you will be astounded. You will not have any recollection that you—when you were a certain age or in a certain cycle—had so many things revealed to you and you understood so much.

"The very same words that you write will be to you like a revelation in ten years, and they will be a revelation because the cup will be widened and it will contain greater energy. When you look back in your diary or your book of your soul communion, you will see the same words and you will say, 'How could it be that I knew so much then?' And of course the same words just keep on growing. They grow with the Tree of Life within you."

That's how the teaching is. It just grows and grows within you in the warmth of Mother's love.

Breviaries

I

The Way of Prayer
by Jesus Christ

1. Unbroken Communion   4

The reality of God is best known by unbroken communion. Adam lost communion. The infinite love of the Creator continues through the span of prodigality. He who extends consciousness as a pure stream of hope unto God. Accepting Jesus' love. Evolution is discerned in the spiritual octaves and in the evolving soul. Comfort is found in the progressive acceptance of universal values. Men must strive to throw off those disquieting attitudes of self which veil the Christ. Those who let flow of the native stream of God's consciousness and love through the aperture of self. Eternal home in the realities of heaven. I AM come to blaze the light of God's undying reality unto all! The way of the Christ is total communion. Jesus begins an effort of world service. Lowering into manifestation the City of God among men. Let brotherhood increase. Hope. The regeneration of the Son of God comes full cycle.

2. Unceasing Prayer   8

"He who seeks to save his life shall lose it." Unceasing prayer. Only as God can live in man does man possess eternal life. The chalice of individuality must expand. It is unnecessary to struggle to achieve communion with God. Renewing strength. The extroversion of human thought depletes energy. A limitless flow of divine strength as you use divine

N.B. Breviary: L breviarium: a brief account or summary; abridgment prayer. The prince of this world will often create a division in your mind. When your energy level is extremely low the forces of negation rush in. The natural two-way flow of consciousness can be achieved through holy communion with God. You can bathe the disquieted energies in your world with the harmony of God. Bringing your iniquities to heaven for judgment. When you keep your problems to yourself often they are intensified. The attempt of evil spirits to flagellate the Deity. Bringing to the Father *all* of one's energy for purification. "Go, and sin no more." Man is accountable for that which he creates. Ordinary prayer is not to be compared with that steadfast outreach for God that understands communion.

3. Holy Prayer   14

The way of the resurrection is the way of God living in man. Fear of birth could well be more justifiable than fear of death. The divine plan of renewing life either through reembodiment or the ascension. Immortal life can be retained only by the Godly. Unbroken communion is the door. To be a friend of God, you must commune with him. The Source will not refuse to answer you. It is not the will of God that any should perish. The abundant life is the natural life. God speaks all day long. There is no end to inspiration and consecration. I AM the flame of resurrection. To be a God, true faith in plan must all expand. Prayer is a ladder to God. The safeguards of holy prayer. Never fear the expansion of divine attunement. The human tendency, after one has risen to great heights, to seek mortal comfort through a rapid descent to degrading lows. Protections of one's spiritual momentum. Those who weary of well doing often undo the good that they have done. Those at inner levels who pray with you will help you in your descent when outer pressures make demands upon your attention. The life of more abundant prayer is a means to a beautiful end. The tendency of men who achieve attunement with God to become overly confident. Performing the work of Christ, the illuminator, and of the intensifier, the Holy Spirit. The fire that shall try every man's work. Prayer without ceasing is the key to streams of God-energy. To seek for the regeneration of God in you is the means of overcoming.

4. The Light of Prayer   22

The light of prayer surges through all things. The light of prayer serves as the communicator between man and God. Developing the sense of an untouchable being. The light is your obedient servant. Your mortal role is played out upon the passing scene that leads you to reality in yourself. Men suppose that their reality is wedded to mortal conditions. The divine flame within is extinguished through neglect. There is only one way—the indivisibility of the Spirit. No outer condition has any power to alter the immortal God flame on the altar of your heart. Consciousness is possessed of a heart. You are able to tune in with the God consciousness that is in every cell of your body and your mighty I AM Presence. The beauty of the Eternal is a permanent one. Men open the door to eternal life by consciously willing themselves free to be that which God created them to be. Every lifestream was given the glorious mantle of ever-present perfection. I AM come that they might have light, and that more abundantly. The selfsame Spirit worketh in all to produce the miracle of communion. Communion is the full measure of salvation to every living soul. In his flesh man may see his flesh as the doorway into the Eternal. The soul may have scars best removed by application to the immortal Spirit of divine reality. Have faith. The habitat of God is in the heaven of man within you. Ever-present opportunity as hope.

5. Prayer as Communication with Purpose 28

Prayer must be regarded as communication with purpose. The world hungers for purity and lingers in guilt. Once the love of God is rightly understood, reality cannot be denied. Christian palliatives have reduced the effectiveness of Jesus' Palestinian mission. The via dolorosa. To make your calling and election sure, you must commune with reality, humility, and absolute sincerity. Faith requires the fuel of fervent effort and fervent communion. Men identify with themselves outwardly and cease recognition of the heavenly image. The heavenly image is the thought God used to fabricate a perfect man. Holy Spirit manifest in men. There is a need in America and in the world to renew the diligent application of prayer. Scientific achievement. The voices of the night are heard and the voices of the day are stilled. The passing moment is an opportunity for bringing about increased good. With God-speed valiant assistance must come forth to men. The work that The Summit Lighthouse seeks to do must be implemented. Hierarchy seeks to teach the lost art of communion with God. The edict that confused the people's speech in the days of the Tower of Babel. The Great White Brotherhood is calling the council of the elect to a vigil of holy prayer. In the span of a few short years men do not learn all of the manifold mysteries of God. Heaven and God are real, tangible, and powerful. God gave to man free will in order that he might create reality within himself. Prayer and communication are the requirements of the day. Decree to "out" the darkness in all men and to radiate the light of love to one another. The art of weaving

the golden flow of the shuttle of attention between
man and his God. "Behold, the Bridegroom cometh!"

6. Universal Prayer   34

The perfect life descending from God has been
strained by mortal misqualification. Stains are
blotted out by the effulgence of the greater light of
the indwelling Christ. The universal Christ raiseth
all upon the ladder of progressive reality. Doctrines,
dogmas, and entrenched concepts have drained
mankind of strength and made him a victim of
satanic myth. The reality of the Christ is the leaven
of truth that serves to elevate consciousness toward
service in the light. Malicious intent. Antichrist has
already come and is in the world. Good is one, and
that oneness is good. The body of Christ on earth can
best be activated in universal harmony. Let men see
all men as brothers. The ascension in the light is a
progressive achievement. By prayer men can attain
oneness with God and reunion of souls. Universal
prayer is a hymn, a wave of light, manchild
manifesting. My rising soul hears the universal
sound. Where God is, there I AM, and everywhere's
my prayer. Attainment comes as seed of God right
within thyself. Expand and know the fullness of the
inner light. True integration with Eternal Law is the
master plan.

7. Continual Prayer   42

True prayer is a cornucopia. Excess anticipation of
self-good without self-surrender drains spiritual treasure and prevents manifestation. Life as an opportunity to become Godlike. The man who does for
himself what others expect God to do for them
will find the abundant life. All substance is one
and all power is one. The granting of a release of

unparalleled strength. The nature of the Father is
within the Son. Allowing the unbroken prayer of
steadfast purpose to act. The building of man's sense
of individuality and perception. It is necessary to prepare through cosmic study to grasp universal principles. The conveyance of thought matrices calculated
to develop an inward approval of the consciousness
of the Creator. Those who claim to be of the eternal
craft of builders and are not. Critics whose criticism
denies the fruit of progress to themselves. Unless the
Spirit lives behind the Word, the flesh is as grass.
Evoke God by continual prayer. Entering into the
One. A pseudocult of religious seekers claiming a
sovereign superiority. Our will, as God's will, is one.
Learn to become the arbiter of your own destiny.
New ideas are the old truths that have always lived in
the universe. Man himself has cast stones of stum-
bling in his brother's pathway. Life is continual.
Unbroken communion transfers the joy of the Lord.
In all things God *is*. God sings the song of the new
day.

II
The Way of Meditation
by Kuthumi

The miracle of attunement is many-sided. Prayer and
meditation are like twins. Meditation is for purification. In prayer man makes intercession to God
for assistance: in meditation he gives assistance
to God. After forgiveness must come the re-creation
of the Divine Man. The image of God has been
vouchsafed to every man. God has proposed; man
has rejected. To meditate is to let the thoughts of God
that flow into the heart rise into the head. Meditation
is an exchange. As man draws the perfection of God

into his world, he becomes as God is—self-created and creating. The alchemy of meditation is to change the *dust* of man's world into the *destiny* of the Eternal. Out of the pure white light of the Christ can be drawn forth the many colors of universal perfection. Meditate upon the relationship of the colors of the rainbow of light's perfection: blue, yellow, pink, white, green, purple and gold, and violet. Transcendence is the nature of the light. Redemption draweth nigh.

10. Plunging into the Ocean of God   72

Meditation takes many forms. Meditation must be entered with a willingness to go where God goes. Ignorant men impute to new religion the responsibility for disturbing men's minds. The fruit is in the very bud of aspiration. Aspire to the highest in your meditations. Meditation carried on by sound and unsound minds. Observations and requirements in the practice of the art of meditation—(1) obtain the sense of one's self, (2) quiet vibratory conditions, (3) begin the process of feeding upon the divine ideal, (4) still the mind and reexamine one's motive. All that is received in one's private meditations is not intended to be copied down and made into a set of academic rules to govern the spiritual enfoldment of others. That which is required of one may not be required of another. Meditation is to quiet the storms that rage in the personal self. "Lord, make me an instrument of thy peace." Radiating attainment softly, imperceptibly into the universe. The disciple must learn the art of graciously identifying with God. The power of example is the strongest bond that speaks of the Most High having descended to mankind. Meditate with the idea of plunging into the ocean of God! Meditation is mediation between God and man! Your thoughts must become chalices into which God can place the truth about himself. Through meditation veils will be removed one by one.

11. A Journey into the Temple Most Holy 80

The posture of men in meditation is examined. Prayers and decrees prior to meditation will insulate, protect, and harmonize the four lower bodies. A period of meditation is regarded as a journey into the Temple Most Holy—the laboratory of the Spirit. Man is dual. Within the id of the lower self must be anchored the bond upon which God depends for the fulfillment of individual creation. Labor in the Temple Most Holy is needed to prove and improve the relationship of the individual to the Higher Self. Entering the Temple Most Holy: come as you are. Each meditation period is intended to enfold you in the character of God. Avoiding the sin of unrighteousness. Yours is the role of the humble child in the crèche. Be willing to endure any suffering for Christ's sake, for God's sake, and for man's sake. The purpose of meditation is that God above may manifest in man below. The strength of divine unity in the body of God upon earth is the requirement of the hour. Learn the path of humility. The greatness of the light belongs to all. The Brotherhood is concerned with the consciousness of service. Not all are called or elected to the same office. Preparation for progress is needed. Clothing the old mysteries. True knowledge is power.

12. The White-Hot Heat of Meditation 88

The eternal Spirit ever seeks to provide opportunity for expansion of consciousness. Human nature tends to vacillate. Communion with the higher conveys grace and opens the heart. Meditation is a form of *satsanga*. Balancing the debts to life. The efficient use

of the immaculate conception. Meditation is a time
when life can convey the highest good to the communicant. The meditator should permit the hand of
God to lead him in thought. The human penchant for
the psychic. Childlike simplicity and trust of the
seeker. God conveys a specific motif to each monad.
The soul that is receptive to the Eternal Fount. In the
Presence of God man enjoys total immunity from the
world and the protection of the light. The purpose of
meditation is to keep man centered in the Presence.
Error intrudes through the ego and through the
rebellion of the children of darkness. Some have lost
their souls through missed opportunities and the
failure to recognize the perspective of reality for
themselves. The consciousness must be prepared in
order to meditate properly. Meditation upon God is
the naturalness of cosmic law. The immutability of
divine law and fervor of the soul generate a white-hot
heat. Hope. The eternal order of universal purpose.
The nature of God is to change the old by the outworking of the Infinite within the finite.

13. Merging with the Impenetrable Light
    of the Atom   94

One of the most difficult things to do is to become
still. When man hotly pursues the Divine, he is not
utterly free to storm the bastions of heaven. The
purpose of the divine romance. The imitation of
Christ is the highest love to which the chela can
aspire. Too often in meditation the feeling of bliss
becomes a trap. The constancy of right meditation.
The greater light must burst the bonds of shadowed
substance, of wrong thought and feeling. God is
available. If man would receive all that is real, he
must give up all that is unreal. The tangibility of God
is the tangibility of his manifestation within. No
mission is greater than the mission of unity with

God. Merging with the impenetrable light that is within the heart of every atom. Prayer is invocative; meditation is convocative. The seeker for truth will find it within. That there is no higher religion than truth must be proven through the science of meditation. The Universal Mind. Meditate in order to bring to God the fruits of your own experience.

14. Universal Light Carries Man to the Altar of Transmutation   100

"If the hill will not come to Mahomet, Mahomet will go to the hill." The temptation to feel bored with life during meditation. The carnal mind says that this "boredom" could be relieved by travel in search of God. God will come to you. Merge with the light. Universal light carries man to the altar of transmutation. There is enough of God to go around. Either your God Presence is sufficient for the day's evils or you must let the world be your teacher. Let men no longer whine, but commune. Do not qualify your aspirations with immortality before they are tried by the fires of God's love. Service must be offered generously without thought of reward or personal glamour. The law of sweet surrender. Surrender under guard. Love. The God-passion caught up in the Macrocosm evokes its responses in the microcosm of men's hearts. "And as ye would that men should do to you, do ye also to them likewise" reveals the justice of God. God made you in his own image that you might express that image in the here and now. As men give, so shall they receive. Universal law picks up in the silent meditations of men's hearts every fear, doubt, and frustrating sense. All that belongs to God is within one's outreach. Let your aspirations soar to the realms of universal ascended master love. Where your desire is, there do your energies flow.

The fashions of meditation may vary. A means
whereby meditation can unfold and expand the
boundaries of individual reality. Every devotee who
yearns to find the happiness of divine reality must
take into account past sowings. Nothing will help so
quickly as to move forward in the light. "But many
that are first shall be last; and the last shall be first."
Throw off the packs of troubles daily. Extend
benefits of daily meditations to a world. Many good-
hearted people are bound in ignorance. Appeals to
God for wisdom. Opportunity of today promises a
beautiful tomorrow. Those who deny the existence of
the material world. Works of imperfection exist
through misunderstanding and error. The carnal
mind ever seeks a means of escape from responsibility and reality. "How much of God can you draw
down into the chalice of self? How much can you
give away?" When you deal with the energies of God
you are dealing with the limitless treasury of Infinity.
Cosmic kinetics. You provide the avenue for the
open door of God's consciousness into the world.
There is no power save that derived from God. The
power of a heart of love. "From the unreal lead me to
the real." God is the portion of every man who will
receive him. The thoughts of God are thoughts of
light. Except ye be born again, ye cannot see the
kingdom of God. Every burden is light: It must go
free!

Awake in God this hour. Come into the Temple of
Interior Illumination. Enter into thy great divine
reality. The Brothers of the Holy Order of Saint

Francis walked as in a cloistered consciousness. The longing of the soul to find entrance into spiritual fortresses of light. This night, by divine permission, you are called apart into a holy and cloistered seclusion. Insulate yourselves in the temple and citadel of your own being. Accept the amplification of virtue. Consciousness is one. God enters the heart of the faithful. Forsake outer consciousness. Behold a flickering flame of being enshrined upon a mighty altar of light. A cup of divine compassion. Give to mankind freedom to accept holy truth and the goodness of your love. Drink into God's peace. The eye of the hurricane of God's wondrous peace. The sunburst of the being of God. The feeling of the Holy Spirit. The emotional body of man must feel a release of all tensions. Cast forth from your being all burdens. A permanent healing if you stand in faith. Assist in the great harvest of souls. God responds to mankind. Elevation of soul must come. That which men see is but a portion of that which you shall externalize. Revelations which you dare not communicate to mankind. A habitation of the vast Spirit of the Universal Architect. Not a poverello, but the richest of all. No one can forge their way into the eternal kingdom. Offer each "jot and tittle" of the law unto God. The Interior Temple of thy existence is builded around thee. The crown of Prince Michael. You have an opportunity. The cobbler who was mocked because he insisted upon perusing the scriptures. Release every wrong thought in your heart and around your emotional being. God shall steer you around many tormenting situations. God's radiance shining forth from you. Be not aloof to the world. God will make thee an instrument of his peace. Let the Christ image be enthroned. You can never change the pristine image which God holds for all. May you dwell in the House of God forever.

III

The Way of the Science of the Spoken Word
by Saint Germain and El Morya

The power of the spoken Word. The proper use of
decrees. "For by thy words thou shalt be justified and
by thy words thou shalt be condemned." Decrees are
not careless words; they are careful words. Decrees
as letters to God. The salutation of the decree
engages the energies of the ascended masters. The
body of your letter is composed of statements
phrasing your desires, the qualifications you would
invoke, and supplications. The close of your decree is
the sealing of the letter in the heart of God. The
covenant of the square squares the release of power
to accomplish the spoken Word. Group decreeing is
more efficacious on a world scale than individual
decreeing. The good released in answer to the call is
automatically opposed. Rhythm is important in
decrees. The laws governing the manifestation and
distribution of physical light also apply to spiritual
light. "Thou shalt decree a thing and it shall be
established unto thee." Individuals who encounter
decrees for the first time can come under the influence of negative forces. There is a time and a place
for meditation, for prayer, and for decrees. Consciousness is one. The children of Israel brought
down the walls of Jericho by a great shout. The
wrong use of the law involving the power of the spoken Word. Decrees are synthesized manifestations
of the heart flame. Proper decreeing is an art. The
speeding up of decrees. Nature is not always silent.
Use your decrees!

Mankind assume that recorded history cannot be changed. The dispensation for the release of the violet flame came forth from the Lords of Karma because Saint Germain offered his momentum of the violet flame to mankind that they might experiment with the alchemy of self-transformation through the sacred fire. The violet flame has always been used in the retreats of the Great White Brotherhood on the etheric plane. Saint Germain proposed that the use of the violet flame be made available to all mankind. Saint Germain envisioned an "I AM race." A debt of gratitude to the early devotees. The flame sets free the energies of all past misuses of the sacred fire. The call compels the answer. The violet flame comes forth from that aspect of the white light called the seventh ray. The fire begins breaking down particles of substance. Energy registers in all of the four lower bodies. The violet flame loosens dense substance and transforms it into light. The oppression of human bondage melts in the fervent heat. The violet singing flame causes the atoms and molecules of your being to be brought into "pitch" with the keynote of your lifestream. The violet flame forgives, consumes, clears, and equalizes the flow of energy, and propels you into the arms of God. The action of the violet flame. The gift of selfhood. Laying down the lesser self. "TRY" as the sacred formula of being.

It is difficult for the world to fully comprehend invisible actions and activities of the sacred fires of God. The dancing stream of electrons. Transmutation as the flame consumes the negative storehouses of energy in the subconsciousness world. Hidden chambers of astral horror which require transmutation. Many succeed in invoking the violet flame through intercessory prayer. The Holy Spirit and Lord Shiva. Exposure to the divine flames. Self-righteousness and the defense of that righteousness. Hold yourselves in a childlike spirit of obedience to the will of God. Truth is its own best defense. The force of rebellion is chaotic and robs man of his peace. Humanity have misused their spiritual powers and forfeited their adeptship. An adherence to wisdom's ray while latent spiritual powers are exploding. Do not overlook the use of the violet transmuting flame. Curbing the manifestation of negative karma by invoking the consuming power of the Holy Spirit. Commending yourselves unto the laws of infinite perfection manifesting in finite realms. Keep open the doorways of mind and heart to the unfoldment of universal will and purpose. A God Star born in your heart.

20. Message to America
    and the People of Earth
    Saint Germain   **164**

A vision to forge your God-identity. The hosts of the Lord have come through the teachers, prophets, and messengers of the ages. The age of the baptism of the Holy Ghost and of the coming of the violet flame. Freedom as the discipline of liberty under the law of God. Jesus, Saint Germain, and the hosts of the Lord serve as the open door for freedom in America and every nation. It is up to you to claim that freedom. The fallen ones are everpresent as the spoilers to take from you your God-ordained liberty. What is peace without freedom? The law of reincarnation. The goal of true religion is the binding of the soul to God in freedom. The earth is intended to be governed by the souls of light. The goal and the calling of America and every true free nation. A revolution of light. The movement to the God Self within is your salvation in this age. Take ten minutes each day to go within. This is my mantra which I give to you as your initiation into the Aquarian age: "I AM a being of violet fire—I AM the purity God desires." Using the name of God to claim the I AM as God's being and be-ness within you. The nation as the identity of the collective Christ consciousness in this age. *Forge your God-identity!* The threefold flame. The chart of the I AM Presence. The potential to be Christ is with you at the moment of your birth. The sacred fire that lives within you is the Holy Spirit. Not all that was passed from Jesus Christ to the disciples has been recorded for your use. Returning the sacred teaching of Christ through the messenger. Accept your role as the protectors of freedom on earth. America's destiny. Inner communion as the foundation of God-government. Archangel Michael comes for the deliverance. The convergence of the teachings of East and West. A call to the lost tribes of the house of Israel. The violet flame is the color of freedom. A call to Afra and the sons and daughters of Afra. The forging of your Self. Be free of all of the past. Be the watchman on the wall of the Lord and the wall of freedom.

Notes

CHAPTER 1

1. Gen. 3:9.
2. Titus 1:15.
3. 2 Cor. 3:18.

CHAPTER 2

1. Mark 8:35.
2. Mark 1:35; 4:38; Luke 6:12; John 6:15.
3. John 12:31; 14:30; 16:11.
4. The attention of your mind controls and directs the flow of God's energy in your world.
5. 1 Tim. 5:24.
6. John 3:19.
7. John 8:11.
8. Luke 15:11-32.
9. Alfred, Lord Tennyson, *The Passing of Arthur*, line 414.

CHAPTER 3

1. Pss. 16:10.
2. John 11:25.
3. John 3:4.
4. Dan. 6:11, 20.
5. Ezek. 33:11.
6. John 10:10.
7. Matt. 5:44.
8. 1 Cor. 3:13.
9. 1 Thess. 5:17.

CHAPTER 4

1. Matt. 23:11.
2. Matt. 10:28.
3. William Shakespeare, *Romeo and Juliet*, act 2, sc. 2, lines 43-44.
4. Job 19:26.
5. Rev. 7:17; 21:4.

CHAPTER 5

1. Luke 23:28.
2. 2 Pet. 1:10.
3. Gen. 11:1-9.
4. William Shakespeare, *Macbeth,* act 5, sc. 1, line 38.
5. Matt. 25:6.

CHAPTER 6

1. John 8:44.
2. Rev. 2:9; 3:9.
3. 1 John 2:18, 22; 4:3; 2 John 7.
4. John 10:30; 17:20-23.
5. Rom. 8:17.

CHAPTER 7

1. John 6:1-14.
2. Matt. 13:15.
3. 1 Tim. 4:14.
4. Rev. 1:16.
5. Matt. 20:22.
6. Eph. 4:4-6.
7. Isa. 8:14; 1 Pet. 2:8.
8. Rev. 21:4-5.

CHAPTER 9

1. Pss. 19:14.
2. Phil. 4:8.
3. Gen. 37:3.
4. John 19:23.
5. Those who desire to dedicate their lives to unbroken communion may wish to amplify the light in their worlds and their service to humanity by wearing the "color of the day" and by making special invocations on that ray. The daily order of the release of the rays from the heart of the sun should not be confused with the numbers of the rays (one through seven) or with the order of the rays depicted in the causal body of man. See illus. facing p. 200.

CHAPTER 10

1. "Know thyself," inscription at the Delphic Oracle. From Plutarch, *Morals.*
2. A Sanskrit term, approximately meaning illusion. All that is finite and subject to change and decay, all that is not eternal and unchangeable. Misqualified energy.

CHAPTER 11

1. See Chapter 21.
2. Matt. 5:48.
3. Bodhisattva: One who has earned his ascension but renounces reunion with God in order to bring divine illumination and understanding to his fellowmen. He may forgo his ascension for thousands of years or until the last man, woman, or child on earth wins his victory.
4. Matt. 9:12.

CHAPTER 12

1. From the Sanskrit; *sat* means "Being, Essence, Reality"; *sanga* means "association." The literal meaning of *satsanga* is "association with Being"; hence the popular interpretation "fellowship with truth" and "communion with holy men, seekers, or those of high ideals."
2. Isa. 11:9; 65:25.
3. Pss. 91:10.
4. Jude 13.
5. Matt. 16:26; 1 Cor. 9:27.

CHAPTER 13

1. Pss. 46:10.
2. Isa. 61:1; Luke 4:18.

CHAPTER 14

1. Francis Bacon, *Essays, Civil and Moral*, "Of Boldness."
2. Matt. 6:24.
3. Matt. 6:34.
4. 1 Cor. 3:13-15; 2 Pet. 3:10-12. This "fervent heat" shows that the action of transmutation is taking place. The process of the refinement of one's personal energies and consciousness is best accomplished through the consecrated daily use of the violet fire. As the violet fire is invoked, it causes a step-up in the vibration of the electrons whirling about the nuclei of the millions of atoms which compose the body and being of man. As these electrons whirl faster and faster in their tiny orbits, the impurities are thrown off into the violet flame, which then changes, or transmutes, their substance into the original purity of God's energy; for it was God's own energy that man misused to produce these densities (impurities) in the first place.
5. Dan. 3:24-25.
6. Luke 6:31.

7. Job 3:25.
8. Matt. 6:21.

CHAPTER 15

1. Matt. 6:28-29.
2. Matt. 19:30.
3. Luke 7:47.
4. *Aesop's Fables,* "The Hare and the Tortoise."
5. Pss. 23:5.
6. Matt. 2:16; 24:24.
7. Mark 1:7.
8. John 19:11.
9. John 14:3.
10. Brihadaranyaka Upanishad 1.3.28.
11. Pss. 19:14.
12. John 3:3.
13. Matt. 11:30.

CHAPTER 17

1. From the Sanskrit; an invocation in the form of either a brief petition or the repetition of the sacred word "AUM."
2. Matt. 12:36-37.
3. See *Studies in Alchemy* and *Intermediate Studies in Alchemy* by Saint Germain, a complete course on the science of precipitation, published by Summit University Press.
4. Job 22:28.
5. Gen. 1:3.
6. Josh. 6:10-20; Heb. 11:30.
7. Mal. 3:10.
8. Job 37:2-5.
9. John 1:1-3; Heb. 11:3.

CHAPTER 18

1. The letters used to form the words "I AM race" are taken from "A-m-e-r-i-c-a."
2. Saint Germain was embodied as Joseph, the protector of Mary and Jesus, and as the prophet Samuel, affectionately called Uncle Sam as he embodies the spirit of freedom to the American people.
3. 1 Cor. 6:20.
4. Matt. 5:18.
5. Acts 2:3.
6. Saint Germain, *Studies in Alchemy* (Los Angeles: Summit University Press, 1967), p. 88.

CHAPTER 20

1. Abraham Lincoln, *Address at Gettysburg,* 19 November 1863.

2. The flame of Mother is the white light of the base-of-the-spine chakra, the kundalini fire which rises to quicken the centers of God-awareness in man.

3. The Goddess of Liberty is the ascended lady master who holds the cosmic consciousness of liberty for the earth.

4. William Shakespeare, *The Merchant of Venice,* act 4, sc. 1, line 184.

5. Afra is the ascended master of Africa helping the people of that continent to find spiritual and individual freedom through self-mastery in the God flame.

CHAPTER 21

1. Job 22:28.

2. Matt. 26:26-28.

3. Rev. 1:8; 21:6; 22:13.

4. Igino Giordani, *Saint Catherine of Siena* (Boston: The Daughters of St. Paul, 1975), p. 72; Rev. Charles Mortimer Carty, *Padre Pio* (Rockford, Ill.: Tan Books and Publishers, Inc., 1973), p. 5; Johannes Steiner, *Therese Neumann* (Staten Island: Society of St. Paul, 1967), pp. 27, 59-60.

5. Matt. 4:4.

6. Maha Chohan, *Pearls of Wisdom,* 24 July 1966, p. 2.

7. Matt. 28:18.

8. Luke 8:45.

9. John 6:51.

10. Josh. 1:1.

11. Josh. 6:3-20.

12. Isa. 45:11.

13. Rev. 19:15.

14. Rev. 11:5.

15. Rev. 12:9, 11.

16. Isa. 55:11.

17. Heb. 1:3.

18. Mark 4:39.

19. Mark 5:1-13.

20. John 11:41.

21. John 11:43.

22. Mark 5:34.

23. Mark 5:41.

24. Mark 2:5.

25. Mark 2:14.

26. Mark 3:3, 5.

27. Exod. 3:14.

28. John 1:3.
29. Luke 24:13-35.
30. John 11:25.
31. Mark 6:13.
32. John 1:12.
33. Matt. 28:18.
34. Matt. 28:20.
35. Instruction of Jesus Christ to the disciples after the resurrection, read from *Akasha*.
See Gal. 6:7.
36. John 17:6, 11, 12, 26.
37. Joel 2:32.
38. Exod. 3:15.
39. Matt. 5:17.
40. John 6:28, 29.
41. Exod. 3:2.
42. Rev. 12:17.
43. John 17:14, 17.
44. John 1:1-3.
45. Logos [Gk, word, reason, speech, account] 1 : reason or the manifestation of reason conceived in ancient Greek philosophy as constituting the controlling principle in the universe: a : a moving and regulating principle in the universe together with an element in man by which according to Heraclitus this principle is perceived b : a cosmic governing or generating principle according to the Stoics that is immanent and active in all reality and that pervades all reality c : a principle that according to Philo is intermediate between ultimate or divine reality and the sensible world 2 : the actively expressed creative revelatory thought and will of God identified in the prologue of the Gospel of St. John and in various Christian doctrinal works with the second person of the Trinity.
46. John 17:2.
47. John 3:16.
48. John 17:2.
49. John 17:3.
50. John 17:1.
51. Mark 3:29.
52. Dan. 9:27; Matt. 24:15; Mark 13:14.
53. 1 Cor. 3:16.
54. Mark 1:27; 3:11; 5:13; Acts 5:16; 8:7; Rev. 16:13-14.
55. Matt. 3:11.
56. Acts 10:34, 35.
57. Matt. 12:37; Rev. 22:12.
58. Acts 17:28.
59. Matt. 26:28.
60. Jer. 31:32; Heb. 8:7-9.

61. Rev. 14:6.
62. Rev. 14:1-3.
63. John 16:7.
64. Isa. 1:18.
65. John 2:1-11.
66. James 2:19.
67. 2 Pet. 3:10.
68. Matt. 3:11.
69. Rev. 21:1.
70. 2 Pet. 3:10-13.
71. John 5:30; 10:38.
72. 2 Pet. 3:12.
73. Acts 2:20.
74. Gen. 1:28.
75. Djwal Kul, *Intermediate Studies of the Human Aura* (Los Angeles: Summit University Press, 1974), p. 122.
76. Acts 13:41.
77. Matt. 6:10.
78. Gen. 1:3.
79. Acts 2:2.
80. Rev. 1:15.
81. Rev. 22:20.

CHAPTER 22

1. John 1:17.
2. John 1:46-49.
3. John 14:12.
4. Heb. 1:3.
5. John 1:14.
6. John 1:3.
7. Rom. 8:17.
8. John 1:16.
9. Jer. 31:33.
10. Col. 2:9.
11. John 1:9.
12. John 3:16.
13. John 1:12.
14. Phil. 2:5.
15. John 2:7-11.
16. Matt. 21:12.
17. Matt. 5:48.
18. 1 Cor. 15:53.
19. *Great Religions of the World* (Washington, D.C.: National Geographic Society, 1971), front flap.
20. John 12:26.

21. John 14:26.
22. Heb. 13:8.
23. Matt. 10:8.
24. Saint Germain, *Studies in Alchemy* (Los Angeles: Summit University Press, 1974), pp. 1-2.
25. Dictation by Jesus Christ, 18 April 1965.
26. John 10:30.
27. Luke 17:21.
28. John 1:14.
29. Phil. 2:8.
30. John 1:5.
31. Col. 2:9.
32. Rev. 3:8.
33. Rev. 3:11; 22:7, 12.
34. Rev. 19:1.
35. Rev. 1:4.
36. Rev. 7:9, 14.
37. Rev. 3:4.
38. Rev. 5:11.
39. Rev. 14:3.
40. Rev. 19:14.
41. Rev. 19:10.
42. Rev. 12:11.
43. Rev. 3:21.
44. Jesus Christ, *Pearls of Wisdom,* 24 July 1977, p. 142.
45. Rev. 22:20.

CHAPTER 23

1. Matt. 10:34.
2. Eph. 3:8.
3. John 1:12.
4. Dictation by Kuthumi, 2 April 1972.
5. Ibid.
6. 1 Pet. 3:4.
7. Morris Bishop, *St. Francis of Assisi* (Boston: Little, Brown & Company, 1974), p. 168.
8. Dictation by Kuthumi, 13 March 1977.
9. Matt. 4:19.
10. 1 John 3:2.
11. Thomas Stanley, *Pythagoras* (Los Angeles: The Philosophical Research Society, Inc., 1970), p. VIII.
12. Eph. 5:1.
13. Dictation by Kuthumi, 1 July 1977.
14. Ibid.

CHAPTER 24

1. John 8:58.
2. Saint Germain, *Pearls of Wisdom*, 27 July 1975, p. 148.
3. 1 Sam. 3:10.
4. Matt. 2:13.
5. Luke 2:40.
6. Luke 21:19.
7. Mother Mary, *Pearls of Wisdom*, 3 March 1968, p. 37.
8. Saint Germain, *Pearls of Wisdom*, 28 August 1977, p. 171.
9. Rev. 10:7.
10. Matt. 11:15.
11. Dan. 12:1.
12. Saint Germain, *Pearls of Wisdom*, 18 September 1977, p. 181.
13. Manly P. Hall, *The Secret Destiny of America* (Los Angeles: Philosophical Research Society, Inc., 1958), pp. 167-170.
14. Isa. 40:28.
15. Saint Germain, *Pearls of Wisdom*, 24 August 1975, p. 176.

CHAPTER 25

1. Luke 9:20.

CHAPTER 26

1. John 1:9.
2. Rev. 11:3-8.
3. Dan. 12:5.
4. John 1:14.
5. Heb. 8:11.
6. See *Cosmic Consciousness: as the highest expression of Heart* by Lanello, published by Summit University Press.
7. Matt. 26:27-28.

For More Information

Paperback books and audio/video cassette lectures on the Teachings of the Ascended Masters by Mark L. Prophet and Elizabeth Clare Prophet available through Summit University Press.

For information on the Keepers of the Flame Fraternity and Lessons, weekly Pearls of Wisdom, Summit University three-month and weekend retreats, Montessori International private school, preschool through twelfth grade, conferences and seminars, contact Summit University Press, Box A, Malibu, California 90265 (818) 880-5300; Royal Teton Ranch (our 30,000-acre self-sufficient spiritual farm and ranch community), Box A, Livingston, Montana 59047 (406) 848-7381; or write for the address of the community teaching center nearest you.

Index

More, Thomas, El Morya as, *ii, 6,* 247

"More Violet Fire," 200

Morya. *See* El Morya

Moses, as a sponsor of Summit University, 241

Mother: Elizabeth Clare Prophet as, 250; flame of, 170, chap. 20 n.2; fusion of the light of Father and, 309; a haven for the Divine, 147. *See also* Mother flame

Mother flame, 309-10, 312; Initiator of the Disciplines of the, *22. See also* Mother

Mother Mary. *See* Mary, Mother

Motive, healing of impure, 185; for meditating must be reexamined, 74

Mountain, can and does come to man, 100

Movement, straightforward, 92

Mu. *See* Lemuria

Muḥammad, *10, illus., 11. See also* Mohammed

Music: at Crotona, 225; devotees of the greatest classical, 89; in meditation, 80; played by Kuthumi, 224; rock, as a desecration of man's temple, 185; of the spheres, 103. *See also* Keynote

Mysteries: of God are not learned in a few short years, 31; old, clothed in more palatable form, 85. *See also* Mystery; Mystery school(s)

Mystery: of the Incarnation, 207; of joint-heirship with Christ, 207. (*See also* Joint-heirship); of the name of God, 183. (*See also* Name); of the Word of God, 183. *See also* Mysteries; Mystery school(s)

Mystery school(s), 240; at Crotona, 225, 240; inner teachings guarded in, 223; the 'once and future', 227; Summit University as, 241. *See also* Mysteries; Mystery

Name: of God, 178, 179, 180, 181-82, 183, 185, 187; instruction on the, of God, 181

Nanak, Guru, *14, illus., 15*

Nation: as the collective Christ consciousness, 167; goal and calling of every free, 166. *See also* Nations

Nations: saving of the, 168; sponsor of the, 167; the voice of conscience of, 226. *See also* Nation

Nature: faith and wisdom of God in, 68; is not always silent, 144; power over, 159

Nimoy, Leonard, 234

Nirvana, each year a certain number attain to, 84

Not-self, replacing the, 216. *See also* Ego; Lesser self; Lower self; Self

Nürnberg, 223

"O Saint Germain, Send Violet Flame," 195-96

"O Violet Flame, Come, Violet Flame!" 198

Old age, dissolving the laws of death and, 187

One: Law of the, 182, 183; from the many the, 45. *See also* Oneness

Oneness: with God, 36; is Good, 35; law of your soul's, with the Spirit, 214; which Jesus exemplified, 183. *See also* One

Open door: to the ascension of the Chinese people, *26;* of Guru, *28;* Jesus as, *i,* 165, 234; which no man can shut, 165

Opinion(s): fear not the, of men, 144; forcing, upon others, 75-76; the shifting sands of mortal, 88

Opportunities, fullest use of life's, 89. *See also* Opportunity

Opportunity: to bring forth genius, 171; to know the Self as God, 168; the star of ever-present, 26; three-dimensional, 177. *See also* Opportunities

Opportunity, Goddess of, extends a

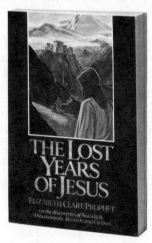

Beloved Sons and Daughters of God,

When Isaiah prophesied the coming of the Messiah, he gave to us the key of the Coming Revolution in Higher Consciousness. He said, "Behold, a virgin shall conceive, and bear a son, and shall call his name Immanuel." According to the sacred mysteries taught by Jesus Christ, this Virgin is the consciousness of the Mother within you—the Mother flame—who immaculately conceives the Son, your own Real Self, by the sacred fire of the Holy Ghost, the veritable threefold light of the Word sent by "our Father who art in heaven."

Truly it is the fusion of the light of our heavenly Father and our earthly Mother which gives to us the Great Synthesis of the Christ consciousness and the anointing of the Holy Ghost in this hour of our soul's victory and our soul's liberation.

The flame of Aquarius is upon us. It is the flame of freedom focused by the Ascended Master Saint Germain, hierarch of the new age. He teaches us that we are born to be God, just as Moses spoke to the children of Israel and said, "Know ye not that ye are gods."* To be God we must know him as the Trinity of Father, Son, and Holy Spirit. But in order to know him in the fullness of that threefold light of power, wisdom, and love, we must first discover the Mother flame within.

This is the flame that I first adored and then became only that I might give you what God has

*Pss. 82:6.

placed in my heart—the law and the principle of Father, the discipline of wholeness in the wisdom of the Son, and the gifts and graces of healing and holiness out of the Holy Spirit.

This is the age when our souls, as the feminine potential of being in man and woman, must make contact with God through the Mother light. The ascended masters, who are our elder brothers and sisters on the path of initiation in higher dimensions of being, are our ever-present teachers who are showing us step-by-step how to do just that. They are the real gurus of the Aquarian age. And they are stepping through the veil in the power of the spoken Word in the dictations which they have given through their messengers not only in this century, but wherever the people Israel have gathered on the face of the earth to "hear the Word of the Lord."

Truly the days spoken of by the prophet Joel are come to pass in which the Lord God is fulfilling his promise, "I will pour out my Spirit upon all flesh...that whosoever shall call on the name of the Lord shall be delivered." At the same time, we see all around us the signs of the end times which Jesus described in chapter 24 of the book of Matthew, signifying that the end of the age of Pisces is upon us and the rising sun of a new order of the ages is about to appear.

Out of the white-fire core of being, the very atom of Selfhood focused in the heart of the sons and daughters of God, comes forth the energy of the Word. It is a spiral of consciousness. It is the revolution of worlds within and worlds without. It signifies the merging of the Macrocosm and the microcosm of being. It is the very energy which transports the soul out of the bondage of time and space and the laws of mortality into new life through the cycles of rebirth inaugurated by the Saviour Jesus Christ and fulfilled in every age by his co-workers and cohorts of light.

All of the sons and daughters of God who have returned to the Father—revealed to Moses in the flaming Presence of the I AM THAT I AM—through the open door of the Christ consciousness are one with Jesus Christ as servants of the Most High. They are the saints of East and West robed in white, moving in and through and among us in these latter days. These ascended masters are calling us Home. Their commanding presence of Life, not death, impels us to accept the challenge to replace human injustice with divine justice, to right every wrong, and to release the love of God that burns in our hearts for the transmutation of all hatred, fear, and torment, and the manifold illusions that separate the souls of earth's evolutions from their oneness with the love of the Promised Comforter personified in the ever-present gurus—the ascended masters.

Sons and daughters of God, I send to you the message of the Coming Revolution and I plead with you before the altar of Almighty God to hear the voice of the Son of God within you and live! We have much to do to be about our Father's business and especially to care for the little children and our youth whose bodies, souls, and minds suffer daily the crucifixion of Christ by the manipulation of the fallen ones. I call you to the Lord's harvest; for as he said, the harvest of souls is truly great but the laborers are few. I call you above all to find your Self and to know that Self as the Great God Self of all, and then to draw forth the energy of your Real Self by the science of the Word and use it not only for the healing of the nations, but also for the healing of these little ones who need our caring today more than ever before.

May the wonderful teachings of the Brotherhood of Light made available through The Summit Lighthouse, the publisher of the teachings of the ascended masters, be for you a soul journey and the answer to the prayer of the Bṛhad-āraṇyaka Upaniṣad that has long been my own: "From the unreal lead me to the real./ From darkness lead me to light./ From death lead me to immortality." And then may these teachings of the Eternal Christ and the adoring Buddha enable us by free will, by love, to fulfill his prayer, "Father make them one, even as we are one."

My beloved, let us be one in the Coming Revolution in Higher Consciousness through the Great Synthesis of the Mother Flame. And let our oneness be for the victory of a planet and a people!

I am forever yours
on the path of soul liberation,

Elizabeth Clare Prophet

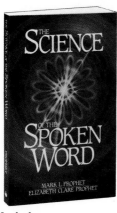

For more information on this summer's Summit University Retreat at the Royal Teton Ranch—survival seminars, wilderness treks, teachings of Saint Germain, dictations from the ascended masters, dynamic decrees, prophecy on political and social issues, personal initiation through the messenger of the Great White Brotherhood, meditation, yoga, the science of the spoken Word, seminars on personal and planetary astrology, children's program, Glastonbury, a self-sufficient spiritual community, summer camping and RV accommodations—call 406/848-7381 or write Royal Teton Ranch, Box A, Corwin Springs, Montana 59021 U.S.A.

SUMMIT UNIVERSITY 🜛 PRESS®

BOOKS IN PRINT

Available through your local bookstore or directly from the publisher, Summit University Press, Dept. 206, Box A, Malibu, CA 90265. To cover postage please add $1.00 on purchases up to $10.00; $1.50 on purchases over $10.00